CONFLICT RESOLUTION GUIDEBOOK FOR MANAGERS

Essential Skills for Preventing, Managing, and Resolving Conflict in the Workplace

AMBER PRESTON

Table of Contents

Introduction

Two team leaders sit across from each other in the conference room, tension hanging thick in the air. A project deadline looms, and both are adamant their approach is the right one. The conversation escalates, leaving their colleagues anxiously looking to their manager for direction. Yet, the manager hesitates, unsure of how to mediate the growing conflict. This scenario is familiar to many workplaces, where conflict lurks in the corners of every meeting room.

The purpose of this book is straightforward: to equip managers like you with the necessary skills to prevent, manage, and resolve workplace conflicts effectively. Conflict is not just an occasional issue; it is a significant part of office life. Studies show that managers spend about 25% of their time dealing with conflicts. This affects productivity, morale, and even the bottom line. The need for effective conflict management has never been more pressing.

This book is structured around practical skills that are vital for any manager aiming to foster a harmonious work environment.

Whether you are a seasoned leader or a new manager, the insights and strategies provided here are designed to elevate your ability to handle conflicts with confidence and competence. This is not a theoretical text filled with jargon. Instead, it offers practical and applicable content that you can implement in your daily work life.

By the end of this book, you will enhance your leadership skills and improve team dynamics. You'll gain increased confidence in handling conflicts, transforming them from obstacles into opportunities for growth and understanding. These essential skills will help you build a more cohesive team, where employees feel valued and understood.

My personal motivation for writing this book stems from my own experiences in management. Early in my career, I found myself in a similar situation to the one described above. I was managing a team with diverse personalities and perspectives. Conflicts arose frequently, and I often felt overwhelmed. It was through trial, error, and learning from experienced mentors that I discovered effective conflict management strategies. This has ignited my passion for helping others navigate similar challenges.

Let's embark on this journey together, armed with the tools and insights needed to make your workplace not just a space of productivity, but a community of collaboration and respect.

ONE

Mastering Effective Communication

E very day, countless managers across the globe make a critical mistake: they hear, but they do not listen. In the midst of workplace noise, genuine communication often gets lost. Consider this - a bustling office where Jane, a project manager, is swamped with emails, phone calls, and back-to-back meetings. An employee approaches her, visibly distressed, with a conflict brewing between team members. Her mind still on the last meeting, Jane nods absentmindedly, offering quick, generic advice before moving on. The employee leaves, feeling unheard and more frustrated. This scenario plays out in many workplaces, leading to unresolved conflicts and a dip in team morale. The crux of the issue often lies in a lack of effective communication, particularly the art of active listening. This is a skill that can transform mere interactions into meaningful dialogue.

1.1 The Art of Active Listening

Active listening is more than just nodding along while someone speaks. It involves a conscious effort to understand the speaker's message, considering not just their words, but their tone, body language, and the context in which they speak. This nuanced form of communication is crucial for managers, as it fosters trust and can lead to more effective conflict resolution. When you listen with the intent to reply rather than understand, you risk missing the core issues at hand. A manager who jumps to respond may inadvertently dismiss important details, making the speaker feel undervalued. Instead, by focusing on comprehension, you can create a space where employees feel safe to express themselves, leading to more productive and harmonious workplace dynamics.

A compelling case study illustrates this principle. In a heated meeting, a manager named Tom faced two employees locked in a bitter disagreement. Instead of choosing sides or offering immediate solutions, Tom engaged through active listening. He reflected on each employee's concerns in his own words, ensuring they felt heard. By paraphrasing and summarizing, Tom not only clarified the core issues, but also defused the tension in the room. This simple act of reflection showed the employees that their perspectives were valued, paving the way for a collaborative solution. Paraphrasing and summarizing are powerful techniques that not only reinforce understanding but also validate the speaker's emotions and viewpoints.

Silence is a powerful tool often overlooked in the art of listening. By allowing a pause after a statement, you create space for deeper reflection and further elaboration. Yes, silence can be uncomfortable, but it serves as an invitation for the speaker to continue, often revealing more than they initially intended. For instance, in a team meeting, pausing after a colleague's comment might encourage them to expand on their thoughts, leading to richer discussions and new insights. Strategic silence becomes a catalyst for more meaningful dialogue, allowing you to glean insights that might otherwise remain hidden.

Avoiding common active listening pitfalls is essential for fostering effective communication. One common error is interrupting, a habit that can derail conversations and breed frustration. Another is making assumptions, which can lead to misunderstandings. Practicing patience and exercising self-restraint in meetings are crucial.

To improve your listening abilities and avoid these common mistakes, consider engaging in workshops or seminars focused on active listening, which can provide a structured environment for skill development. Role-play scenarios can be invaluable for honing these skills. By simulating real-life conflicts, managers can practice the discipline of listening without interjecting, cultivating a more patient and attentive demeanor that enhances team interactions. Feedback loops, where team members offer insights into each other's listening effectiveness, can also illuminate areas for improvement. Through practice and reflection, you will begin to transform your listening from a passive to an active skill, strengthening your leadership capabilities even further.

1.2 Assertive Communication for Clarity

Assertive communication is the backbone of clear and respectful workplace interactions. It is a skill that can transform the way you engage with your team. Assertiveness involves expressing your thoughts, feelings, and needs directly and respectfully, fostering an environment where everyone feels heard and respected. Unlike aggressiveness, which bulldozes over others to achieve personal goals, assertiveness seeks balance. It allows you to stand your ground while considering the perspectives and feelings of others. This balance clarifies your intentions and encourages a culture of mutual respect. In the fast-paced environment of modern workplaces, the ability to communicate assertively is invaluable. It empowers managers to navigate conflicts with confidence and poise, reducing misunderstandings and fostering a more collaborative atmosphere.

Developing assertive communication starts with understanding its core components. One effective framework involves crafting assertive messages that articulate your needs and expectations without assigning blame. "I" statements are particularly useful here. For example, instead of saying, "You never listen to my ideas," an assertive approach would be, "I feel overlooked when my ideas are not considered during discussions." This subtle shift in language focuses on your feelings and experiences, reducing defensiveness and opening the door for constructive dialogue. It's also crucial to clearly state your needs and expectations. Instead of vague requests, be specific about what you require and why it matters. This clarity helps others understand your perspective and sets the stage for more effective problem-solving. By consistently using these techniques, you can foster a more transparent and cooperative work environment.

However, despite its benefits, assertive communication presents challenges for many managers. One common hurdle is the fear of conflict or rejection. Many people shy away from assertiveness, worried they might upset others or face backlash. But, avoiding assertiveness can lead to passive communication, where important issues remain unaddressed, ultimately breeding resentment. Overcoming this fear requires a shift in mindset. Recognize that assertive communication is not about being confrontational; it is about being clear and honest. Building confidence in your ability to express yourself assertively can be achieved through practice and reflection. Consider why you hesitate to speak up and challenge those fears with positive affirmations or support from peers. As you gradually build confidence, you will find that assertiveness leads to more fruitful and respectful interactions.

This is another area where role-playing scenarios can offer a safe environment to practice assertiveness without the pressure of real-world consequences. Imagine a scenario where a team member frequently interrupts others during meetings. In a role-play, practice addressing this behavior assertively by saying, "I notice that interruptions are frequent, and I feel it hinders our team's ability to collaborate effectively. Can we establish a protocol to ensure everyone has a chance to speak?" This will help you refine your language and approach, making you more prepared for real situations. The role-play sessions can be organized within your team or with a mentor, providing feedback and insights to enhance your communication style. By regularly engaging in these exercises, you reinforce your ability to communicate assertively, making it a natural part of your interactions.

Assertive communication is more than a skill; it is a mindset that transforms workplace dynamics. It encourages openness, reduces conflict, and fosters a culture of respect and understanding. As you integrate these practices into your daily interactions, you will notice a shift in how your team communicates and collaborates. Assertiveness empowers you to articulate your needs clearly and respectfully, paving the way for more effective conflict resolution and stronger team relationships.

1.3 Non-Verbal Cues and Their Impact

In any conversation, what you say often carries less weight than how you say it. Non-verbal communication plays a pivotal role in reinforcing or undermining verbal messages. It's not just the words that matter; it's the posture you maintain, the gestures you use, and the facial expressions you exhibit. These elements can convey confidence or insecurity, openness or defensiveness, and they do so without a single word being spoken. Consider a manager who delivers a positive performance review while maintaining a slouched posture and avoiding eye contact. Despite the glowing feedback, their body language might suggest indifference or insincerity, leaving the employee confused and undervalued. Recognizing the power of non-verbal cues is crucial for effective communication, especially in managing conflicts where the subtleties of body language can either calm the storm or fan the flames.

To become adept at interpreting these signals, start by paying close attention to the body language of those around you. Subtle signs can speak volumes. For instance, crossed arms may indicate defensiveness, while a lack of eye contact might suggest discomfort or dishonesty. Recognizing these cues can provide valuable insights into an employee's state of mind during conflicts. You can use this awareness to tailor your approach, addressing underlying concerns before they escalate. Understanding these non-verbal signals allows you to navigate conversations with greater empathy and precision, making it easier to address and resolve conflicts effectively.

Managing your own non-verbal communication is equally important. The way you hold yourself in meetings, the expressions you wear, and the gestures you use can influence the outcome of an interaction. Open body language—such as facing the person you're speaking with, uncrossed arms, and a relaxed posture—can foster trust and encourage open dialogue. Similarly, maintaining a facial expression that conveys empathy and attentiveness helps put others at ease, making them more likely to share candidly. This openness is crucial when navigating conflicts. Practicing these skills can improve your ability to communicate non-verbally, ensuring that your actions align with your words and reinforce the message you intend to convey.

In your various role-playing scenarios, be sure to pay attention to your non-verbal communication too. Another effective method is mirror practice. This involves observing your body language in a mirror while speaking, noting any gestures or expressions that might contradict your verbal message. By becoming acutely aware of your non-verbal tendencies, you can make conscious adjustments, aligning your body language with the message you want to communicate. This practice sharpens your self-awareness, while enhancing your ability to interpret and respond to the non-verbal signals of others.

Understanding and mastering non-verbal communication is not just about avoiding miscommunications. It's about creating a workplace where messages are clear, intentions are understood, and conflicts are resolved amicably. This skill set can transform the way you interact with your team, making you a more effective and empathetic leader. As you hone your ability to read and project non-verbal cues, you'll find that your interactions become more productive, your team more collaborative, and your work environment more positive. The subtlety of non-verbal communication might seem challenging at first, but with practice and awareness, it becomes an indispensable tool in your managerial toolkit.

1.4 Managing Emotions During Conversations

Emotions often serve as the unseen force driving conversations. In conflict situations, the ability to regulate these emotions is crucial for managers. Unchecked emotions can quickly escalate a tense situation, turning a manageable disagreement into a full-blown conflict. For instance, imagine a heated discussion about project deadlines. If one person reacts with anger, the ensuing defensiveness from the other can derail any chance of a productive dialogue.

Emotional regulation is not about suppressing feelings; it's about recognizing them and choosing how to respond. This skill allows managers to navigate conflicts with poise, facilitating discussions that lead to resolution rather than escalation.

Recognizing and naming emotions is the first step toward managing them. It involves pausing to identify what you're feeling and why. This self-awareness can prevent emotional reactions from clouding judgment. Consider a manager who feels frustrated during a meeting. By acknowledging this frustration, they can take a moment to breathe and decide on a calmer response. Techniques like emotional labeling, where you put a name to your feelings, can help in maintaining clarity and focus. This practice aids in self-regulation and also sets a positive example for your team, demonstrating that emotions can be managed constructively.

Maintaining emotional balance during difficult conversations requires deliberate strategies. Deep breathing exercises are a simple yet effective tool. By focusing on slow, deep breaths, you can calm your body's stress response, clearing your mind for rational thinking. Another strategy is cognitive restructuring, which involves reframing negative thoughts into more positive or neutral ones. For instance, instead of thinking, "This conflict is a disaster," you might reframe it as "This is an opportunity to find a better solution." These mental shifts can reduce anxiety and prepare you to engage more effectively in conflict resolution. These techniques empower you to remain composed, ensuring that emotional turbulence doesn't overshadow the conversation's goals.

The impact of unmanaged emotions on communication can be profound. Emotional outbursts, such as shouting or sarcasm, often lead to misunderstandings and hurt feelings, making it difficult to reach a constructive outcome. A common example is a manager who, overwhelmed by stress, lashes out at a team member. The immediate effect is a breakdown in trust and communication, with long-term repercussions on team morale. Such scenarios underscore the importance of emotional control in maintaining productive workplace relationships. When emotions go unchecked, they can become barriers to effective communication, creating rifts that take significant effort to mend.

As a manager, you also play a critical role in helping others manage their emotions. Offering a calm presence can be incredibly grounding for employees in distress. By maintaining a steady demeanor, you provide a safe space for them to express their feelings without fear of judgment. By acknowledging their emotions and validating their experiences, you help employees feel heard and supported. Encouraging your team to adopt emotional regulation techniques aids in conflict resolution and also fosters a culture of emotional intelligence. When employees see their leaders model emotional control, they're more likely to emulate these behaviors, leading to a more resilient team.

Interactive Exercise: Building Emotional Awareness

Encourage your team to engage in a reflection exercise to build emotional awareness and emotional regulation. Ask team members to take a moment at the end of each week to reflect on their interactions. What emotions did they notice in themselves and others? How did these emotions influence their communication and decision-making? By consciously reflecting on these experiences, team members can develop a deeper understanding of their emotional landscape and that of their colleagues. This can help strength future conversations between team members.

1.5 Tailoring Communication for Diverse Teams

Navigating the complex landscape of a multicultural team requires more than just general communication skills. It demands a keen understanding of the cultural and individual differences that shape how messages are received and interpreted. In diverse teams, communication isn't merely about exchanging information; it's about bridging gaps between varied cultural contexts. Recognizing these differences is crucial for managers aiming to foster an inclusive workplace. Consider a team made up of individuals from different cultural backgrounds. Each member brings unique perspectives, but also distinct communication styles that can clash if not carefully managed. A one-size-fits-all approach does not work well here, making cultural sensitivity a necessary skill for any manager. Cultural sensitivity training can provide the tools needed to navigate these waters, helping managers understand and appreciate the diverse backgrounds of their team members. By honing these skills, you can create a more collaborative and productive team dynamic.

Effective cross-cultural communication requires deliberate effort and specific strategies. One fundamental approach is to avoid idioms and jargon that may not translate well across cultures. What may seem like a harmless phrase to one person can be confusing or even offensive to another. Instead, opting for clear and simple language ensures that your message is accessible to all. Additionally, understanding communication preferences across cultures is vital. Some cultures value directness, while others may see it as confrontational. By adapting your communication style to suit these preferences, you can create an environment where everyone feels respected and understood, paving the way for more effective collaboration.

Unfortunately, misinterpretations due to cultural differences are common, often leading to conflicts that can derail team cohesion. Overcoming these hurdles require building a culture of inclusivity and respect. Encouraging open dialogues where team members can share their cultural perspectives fosters understanding and reduces the risk of miscommunication. This inclusivity enriches the team dynamic and positions the team to harness the full spectrum of ideas and innovations that diversity brings.

To support managers in developing these vital skills, there are numerous tools and resources available. Diversity and inclusion workshops offer structured environments where managers can learn about different communication styles and how to adapt to them. These workshops often include practical exercises and discussions that enhance cultural awareness and sensitivity. Language and cultural exchange programs are also beneficial. They provide managers with firsthand experience in navigating cultural differences, offering insights that can be directly applied to their teams. By participating in these activities, managers can equip themselves with the knowledge and skills needed to lead diverse teams effectively.

As you integrate these strategies into your management practices, you'll notice a transformation in how your team communicates and collaborates. The effort invested in understanding and adapting to diverse communication needs pays off in a more cohesive and innovative team environment. By prioritizing cultural sensitivity and effective cross-cultural communication, you set the foundation for a workplace where every team member feels valued and heard. This inclusive approach not only enhances team dynamics but also drives the organization towards greater success and growth. Embracing these principles ensures that you, as a manager, are well-prepared to lead in today's diverse and dynamic workplace.

TWO

Emotional Intelligence in Conflict Resolution

C onsider a typical morning at the office, where the hum of productivity is suddenly disrupted by raised voices echoing through the hallway. Two colleagues, usually amicable, are locked in a heated argument over a missed deadline. Their manager is caught off guard and watches helplessly as the situation spirals out of control. These types of scenes are common in workplaces, where emotions often run high and can lead to conflicts if not managed well. Understanding and managing these emotional undercurrents is crucial for resolving conflicts effectively. This is where emotional intelligence comes into play, offering managers a toolkit to navigate and mitigate disputes by recognizing and addressing emotional triggers.

2.1 Understanding Emotional Triggers

Emotional triggers are stimuli that elicit strong emotional reactions, often leading to conflict when unchecked. These triggers can vary widely among individuals and teams. For some, criticism might spark defensiveness, while for others, an overwhelming workload can be the tipping point. Recognizing these triggers is essential in preventing knee-jerk reactions that can exacerbate conflicts. When you identify your own triggers, as well as those of your team, you gain insight into potential flashpoints, allowing you to address issues before they escalate. This proactive approach can transform conflict from a destructive force into an opportunity for growth and understanding.

To identify personal emotional triggers, self-assessment and reflection are invaluable tools. Journaling exercises are particularly effective in this regard. By regularly documenting emotional responses to various situations, you can uncover patterns that reveal your triggers. This allows you to reflect on moments of heightened emotion, noting the circumstances and your reactions. This practice not only fosters greater self-awareness but also empowers you to take control of your emotional landscape. Additionally, seeking feedback from peers can provide an external perspective on behaviors you might be unaware of. Colleagues can offer insights into how your emotions manifest in the workplace, helping you recognize triggers that might otherwise go unnoticed.

Ignoring emotional triggers can have a profound impact on conflict dynamics. Unrecognized triggers often lead to reactive behavior, which can escalate conflicts and create a toxic work environment. Consider a manager whose stress levels spike under tight deadlines. Without acknowledging this trigger, their stress might manifest as irritability, affecting team morale and productivity. Common workplace triggers such as criticism, high workload, or a lack of recognition can create tension if left unaddressed. By bringing these triggers to light, you can develop strategies to manage them effectively, preventing them from undermining team cohesion and performance.

Managing emotional triggers requires intentional strategies to anticipate and mitigate responses. Mindfulness practices are particularly useful here. By cultivating mindfulness, you increase your self-awareness, allowing you to recognize and address triggers before they lead to conflict. Techniques such as deep breathing, meditation, or simply taking a moment to pause and reflect can help you maintain emotional equilibrium. These practices foster a sense of calm and clarity, enabling you to respond thoughtfully rather than react impulsively. By integrating mindfulness into your daily routine, you create a buffer between stimulus and response, allowing you to navigate conflicts with greater ease and effectiveness.

Interactive Exercise: Identifying Your Emotional Triggers

Grab a notebook or piece of paper to try a journaling exercise to identify your emotional triggers. Over the next week, take a few uninterrupted minutes at the end of each day to reflect on moments of intense emotion. Note the situation, your emotional response, and any patterns you observe. Consider what might have triggered your reaction and how you felt in the moment. At the end of the week, review your entries to identify common themes. This reflection will help you understand your triggers better and prepare you to manage them constructively in the future.

2.2 Self-Regulation Techniques for Managers

In the middle of a crisis, a manager's ability to maintain composure can set the tone for the entire team's response. Self-regulation, the ability to manage emotions and impulses, is a cornerstone of effective leadership. When you stay calm and collected, even in challenging situations, you think more clearly and inspire confidence in those around you. This self-control is crucial in creating a stable and productive work environment, where team members feel secure and focused, even when faced with adversity. A manager who demonstrates composure during crises can guide their team through turbulence, ensuring that decisions are made with clarity and purpose rather than under the influence of stress or panic.

There is a strong connection between self-regulation and effective decision-making. When emotions run high, judgment can become clouded, leading to hasty and often regrettable decisions. Self-regulation allows you to step back and assess situations objectively, weighing options with a clear mind. Think about a manager who is faced with a tense meeting where tempers are flaring. By maintaining composure, they can facilitate a more reasoned discussion, guiding the team toward a consensus rather than allowing the situation to devolve into chaos. This ability to stay level-headed not only enhances decision-making but also models effective conflict management for the team, fostering an environment where thoughtful deliberation is valued.

To enhance self-regulation, there are several actionable strategies you can incorporate into your daily routine.

- Breathing exercises are a simple yet powerful way to center yourself. By focusing on slow, deep breaths, you can calm your nervous system, allowing you to regain control over your emotions. Try 'box breathing', where you inhale for 4 counts, hold your breath for 4 counts, exhale for 4 counts, hold your breath for 4 counts, and repeat. This practice is particularly useful in heated discussions, where the temptation to react impulsively can be overwhelming.
- Pausing before responding gives you a moment to consider your words carefully, reducing the risk of exacerbating the conflict. The pause can also serve as a

signal to others that you are thoughtfully engaging with the situation, rather than reacting reflexively. Such mindfulness in communication can lead to more constructive dialogues and effective conflict resolution.

- Daily meditation or reflection sessions are great ways to cultivate self-regulation. Incorporate this into your practice for identifying emotional triggers. Since this practice increases your emotional awareness, by taking it one step further, you can also learn to anticipate and manage your responses more effectively. Over time, these sessions can help you develop a more balanced and resilient mindset. As you make self-regulation a habit, you'll find that your ability to navigate conflicts and make sound decisions becomes second nature, enhancing both your personal and professional life.

2.3 Empathetic Leadership in Conflict Scenarios

Empathy is the cornerstone of effective conflict resolution, acting as a bridge between differing perspectives. In its simplest form, empathy is the ability to understand and share the feelings of another. For managers, this means stepping into the shoes of employees, seeing the world from their vantage point. This connection fosters trust and openness, creating an environment where employees feel valued and understood. It is this atmosphere that paves the way for resolving conflicts amicably. Empathy is not a natural skill for everyone, but it can be cultivated through conscious effort and practice. Emotional intelligence training programs are an excellent starting point. These programs enhance your ability to recognize and regulate your emotions while under-standing those of others, which is crucial in high-stress situations.

Empathetic leadership manifests in various behaviors that you can incorporate into your management style. Consider actively seeking employee input during conflicts. This means not just waiting for feedback, but actively creating spaces where team members feel comfortable sharing their thoughts and concerns. It involves asking open-ended questions and genuinely listening to the responses, acknowledging the emotions and viewpoints expressed. Acknowledging and validating team members' feelings is another critical aspect. This doesn't mean you always have to agree, but it shows respect for their perspective. Verbal affirmations like, "I can see why you feel this way," can go a long way in making employees feel valued and understood.

Developing empathy skills requires intentional and consistent practice. Take a moment and consider these few methods:

- Perspective-taking exercises - Imagine yourself in another person's situation, considering how their experiences shape their reactions. Consider reflecting with colleagues to role-play different scenarios you may have previously encountered.
- Empathy mapping exercises - Systematically analyze a person's thoughts, feelings, and actions in a given scenario. This can help gain a holistic understanding of a person's experience, helping you identify solutions that truly address the person's needs. Consider using a visual mapping method.
- Regular check-ins - These check-ins should go beyond task updates; they should be opportunities to engage in meaningful conversations about how your team members are feeling and any challenges they might be facing. Consider sharing personal stories or experiences that

relate to your team member's struggles to create a sense of camaraderie and mutual understanding.

Overall, these exercises enhance your ability to connect with others on an emotional level, making you more attuned to their needs and concerns. Over time, these practices can shift your natural response to be more empathetic, ultimately leading to stronger interpersonal relationships within your team.

Maintaining empathy in high-pressure situations can be challenging, but is crucial for effective leadership. Stress can often lead to a tunnel vision focus on results, causing leaders to inadvertently neglect the emotional needs of their team. A level of awareness enhances your empathy and fosters a more inclusive and supportive work environment. It is about creating a space where everyone feels heard and valued. When managers prioritize empathy, they lay the groundwork for a more harmonious and collaborative team dynamic. This approach resolves conflicts and also prevents them, as employees are more likely to voice concerns before they escalate.

2.4 Leveraging Emotional Intelligence for Negotiation

Imagine entering a negotiation room with the ability to read the unspoken signals of your counterpart. The subtle shift in their posture, the fleeting glance, or the tone of their voice—all offering clues to their true intentions and emotions. Emotional intelligence plays a pivotal role in negotiation, enhancing your ability to navigate these complex interactions. It's not just about knowing what to say, but understanding how to say it and, most importantly, how to listen. When you tap into your emotional intelligence, you gain a deeper understanding of the other party's needs and desires, allowing you to influence the negotiation dynamics positively. This understanding creates a space where both parties feel valued, leading to mutually beneficial outcomes. By leveraging your emotional intelligence, you can transform a potentially adversarial negotiation into a collaborative dialogue, where trust and cooperation flourish.

Applying emotional intelligence in negotiations involves several key strategies. One important technique is reading emotional cues to gauge the negotiation dynamics. Pay attention to the non-verbal signals that your counterpart is sending. Are they leaning forward, indicating engagement, or crossing their arms, suggesting defensiveness? These observations can guide your approach, allowing you to adjust your tactics in real time. Building rapport is another essential strategy. Establishing a connection with the other party fosters trust, making it easier to reach agreements. Start by finding common ground, perhaps through shared interests or experiences. This rapport eases tensions and opens the door to more honest and productive conversations. When both parties trust each other, they are more likely to collaborate, seeking solutions that benefit everyone involved.

The impact of emotional intelligence on negotiation success is well-documented. Consider this case where empathy led to a win-win solution. Two companies were at odds over a joint venture, each focused on maximizing its own gains. However, when the negotiators began to actively listen and empathize with each other's concerns, the dynamic shifted. By understanding the underlying motivations and pressures each company faced, they were able to craft a solution that addressed both parties' needs. This empathy-driven approach resulted in a partnership that not only met financial goals, but also strengthened their business relationship. This example highlights how emotional intelligence can turn a negotiation from a battleground into a platform for creative problem-solving.

Incorporating emotional intelligence into your negotiation strategy can lead to more successful outcomes. It's a skill that requires practice and reflection, but the benefits are significant. Developing these negotiation-related emotional intelligence skills goes hand in hand with developing empathy. Role-playing negotiation scenarios allows you to practice and refine your techniques in a controlled setting. These activities can also broaden your understanding of how others might feel or think during negotiations, improving your capacity to reach agreements that satisfy all parties involved. Also, by understanding and influencing your counterparts through emotional intelligence, you can navigate negotiations with greater ease and effectiveness.

2.5 Building Emotional Resilience in High-Stress Situations

In the dynamic and often unpredictable world of management, emotional resilience stands as a crucial ally. This resilience is the capacity to recover quickly from difficulties and setbacks, a trait that is indispensable in managing stress and conflict. Think of resilience as the mental elasticity that allows you to remain steady and composed, even when faced with adversity. It's not about avoiding stress or conflict, but rather about being able to bounce back and continue moving forward with clarity and purpose. This ability is fundamental for managers who must navigate the turbulent waters of workplace dynamics, ensuring they can lead effectively even under pressure.

Developing emotional resilience involves a conscious effort to strengthen your mental and emotional muscles. One effective technique is positive reframing, which involves looking at challenging situations from a different perspective. By focusing on what can be learned from a difficult experience rather than dwelling on the negatives, you can transform setbacks into opportunities for growth. This shift in mindset helps in reducing stress, while building a more optimistic outlook. Another strategy is developing a growth mindset, where challenges are seen as opportunities to learn and improve. This mindset encourages embracing difficulties as a natural part of life and work, fostering a resilient attitude. With a growth mindset, setbacks become stepping stones rather than stumbling blocks, allowing you to approach challenges with curiosity and determination.

The benefits of emotional resilience for managers are profound. Resilient managers are better equipped to perform consistently under pressure, maintaining focus and effectiveness even when the going gets tough. This will not only boost personal productivity, but also inspire confidence and stability within the team. When team members see their leader maintaining composure amidst chaos, it sets a powerful example, encouraging them to adopt a similar mindset. This ripple effect enhances the overall resilience of the team, creating a work environment where challenges are met with calmness and resolve. Emotional resilience also supports better decision-making by enabling managers to remain clear-headed and objective, even in high-stakes situations. This clarity ensures that decisions are based on rational thought rather than emotional reactivity, leading to more effective outcomes.

Incorporating resilience-building practices into your daily routine can make the development of this vital skill a natural part of your life. For instance, consider journaling about daily stressors and coping strategies. By taking time each day to reflect on the challenges you faced and how you handled them, you gain valuable insights into your resilience patterns. This reflection helps you identify areas for improvement and reinforces your strengths, boosting your confidence in your ability to cope with future challenges. Over time, this practice can deepen your self-awareness, providing a solid foundation for building emotional resilience.

Additionally, setting aside time for activities that promote relaxation and stress relief, such as exercise or hobbies, can further bolster your resilience by ensuring you have a healthy outlet for stress.

As we conclude this chapter on emotional intelligence, it's clear that these skills are not just about managing conflicts—they're about transforming how we approach challenges. Emotional resilience, self-regulation, and empathetic leadership all contribute to creating a work environment where conflicts are opportunities for growth. In the next chapter, we'll explore how to apply these skills within structured frameworks, providing you with tangible strategies to navigate and resolve conflicts effectively.

THREE

Conflict Resolution Frameworks

E nvision a dynamic workplace alive with energy, where a team of talented individuals is united by a common goal. However, just below this lively surface, tensions brew due to conflicting priorities and communication breakdowns, threatening the spirit of collaboration. The project manager, acutely aware of the growing discord, recognizes that addressing these conflicts is crucial for maintaining team cohesion and productivity. This is where the power of a well-constructed conflict resolution framework becomes evident. By systematically identifying and addressing the root causes of conflict, managers can transform potential disruptions into opportunities for growth and innovation. A structured approach resolves immediate tensions and lays the groundwork for a harmonious and resilient team.

To achieve sustainable conflict resolution, it's essential to distinguish between symptoms and root causes. Symptoms are the visible expressions of conflict—such as arguments or decreased productivity—while root causes are the underlying issues fueling these symptoms. Addressing symptoms alone may provide temporary relief, but true resolution requires a deeper understanding of the core problems. Imagine a manager dealing with frequent arguments over project deadlines. While the immediate issue seems to be time management, the root cause might be a lack of clear communication or unrealistic expectations. By identifying and addressing these foundational issues, managers can prevent future conflicts and foster a more collaborative environment.

3.1 Conducting a Root Cause Analysis

A "root cause analysis" is a powerful tool for uncovering any underlying issues. One effective method is the "5 Whys" technique, originally developed by Toyota for manufacturing, but now widely used in conflict resolution. This approach involves repeatedly asking "why" to peel back the layers of a problem, ultimately revealing the root cause. Start by clearly defining the problem statement, then ask the first "why" to explore surface-level reasons. Continue this process up to four more times, each answer leading to a more in-depth understanding of the issue. This method not only clarifies the problem, but also encourages open dialogue and transparency.

Another valuable tool for root cause analysis is the Fishbone diagram, also known as the Ishikawa diagram. This visual representation helps organize potential causes of a problem into categories, such as people, processes, or technology. By systematically exploring each category, managers can identify patterns and connections that may not be immediately apparent. This structured approach aids in uncovering root causes and facilitates a comprehensive understanding of the conflict, enabling more targeted and effective interventions. By utilizing these tools, managers can get a clear picture of the issues at hand, paving the way for meaningful and lasting resolutions.

Common root causes of workplace conflicts often stem from misaligned goals or priorities. When team members have differing objectives or lack a shared understanding of project goals, tensions can arise. Misunderstandings, whether due to unclear instructions or assumptions, can lead to frustration and resentment. To address these issues, managers must prioritize open and honest communication, creating an environment where concerns can be freely expressed and addressed. By focusing on clearly defining goals and priorities, managers can proactively prevent conflicts and create a more cohesive and productive team dynamic. Regularly check in with your team members to ensure clarity and address any questions.

Gathering information during root cause analysis is crucial for gaining insights into the conflict. Having a one on one conversations with each of the involved parties provides firsthand accounts of the issues, offering valuable perspectives that might otherwise be overlooked. These conversations should be approached with empathy and active listening, ensuring that all voices are heard and respected. Also, reviewing past conflict incidents can shed light on recurring patterns or systemic issues. By analyzing previous conflicts, managers can identify trends and develop strategies to address them effectively. This comprehensive approach not only resolves the current conflict, but also strengthens the team's ability to navigate future challenges with confidence.

Interactive Exercise: Conducting a Root Cause Analysis

To put these techniques into practice, consider conducting a root cause analysis with your team. Begin by selecting a recent conflict or challenge that has affected the team. Use the "5 Whys" technique to explore the underlying issues, encouraging open dialogue and transparency throughout the process. Then, create a Fishbone diagram to visually organize potential causes, involving team members in brainstorming and categorizing each factor. This exercise will help identify root causes, while also fostering a collaborative problem-solving mindset, empowering your team to address conflicts proactively and effectively.

3.2 Designing Resolution Frameworks

Imagine you're tasked with creating a plan that addresses an ongoing conflict and prevents future ones. This plan, or resolution framework, is a structured approach that guides you through the conflict resolution process with clarity and precision. At its core, an effective framework begins with defining clear objectives and desired outcomes. This means knowing precisely what resolution looks like—not just stopping the argument, but ensuring the team aligns on future goals. A good framework also involves stakeholder engagement strategies. This involves identifying who needs to be involved in the resolution process and understanding their interests. Whether it's team members, department heads, or even external partners, knowing who plays a part in the conflict and its resolution is crucial. Their involvement ensures that all perspectives are considered, leading to solutions that are not only fair, but also sustainable.

Creating a resolution framework requires a step-by-step approach tailored to the specific conflict at hand. Start by identifying the stages of conflict. Is it just beginning, or has it reached a peak? Different stages require different interventions. For initial conflicts, you might focus on facilitating open communication to prevent escalation. For more entrenched disputes, mediation or negotiation might be necessary. Once you've mapped out the stages, determine the appropriate interventions for each. This might include scheduled group meetings, workshops, or one-on-one discussions. Incorporating these interventions into your plan ensures that you have a roadmap to guide the conflict through to resolution. This clarity helps in resolving the current issue and equips your team with strategies to handle future conflicts independently.

Flexibility is a crucial aspect of any framework. No two conflicts are identical, and rigid frameworks can hinder resolution efforts. Instead, frameworks should be adaptable, allowing you to adjust your approach as situations evolve. For example, a conflict involving miscommunication in one department may require different tactics than a disagreement over resource allocation in another department. As the conflict progresses, new information may come to light, necessitating a shift in strategy. By building flexibility into your framework, you ensure it remains relevant and effective, regardless of the specifics of the conflict. This adaptability addresses immediate issues and also builds resilience within your team, empowering them to navigate future challenges with confidence.

Another best practice in framework development is involving diverse perspectives in the design process. By bringing together individuals from different backgrounds and roles, you gain a richer understanding of the conflict's context and potential solutions. This diversity of thought can lead to innovative strategies that might not have been considered otherwise. Additionally, engaging a broad range of stakeholders in the design process fosters a sense of ownership and commitment to the resolution. When team members feel their voices are heard, they are more likely to support the framework and its implementation. This collective buy-in is essential for the framework's success, as it ensures that all parties are aligned in their efforts to resolve the conflict.

Keep in mind, developing a resolution framework is not a one-time task. It requires ongoing assessment and refinement based on feedback and outcomes. Regularly reviewing the framework's effectiveness allows you to make necessary adjustments and improvements. This iterative process ensures that the framework remains responsive to the changing needs of your team and organization. It also provides an opportunity to learn from each conflict, using insights gained to enhance future resolution efforts. By prioritizing continuous improvement, you create a framework that not only resolves current conflicts, but also strengthens your team's ability to handle future challenges. This proactive approach fosters a culture of learning and growth, where conflicts are seen as opportunities for development and innovation.

3.3 Implementing Step-by-Step Conflict Resolution

With a conflict resolution framework in hand, the next step is to bring it to life in your organization. Implementation requires careful planning and execution, starting with clearly assigning roles and responsibilities. Each team member should know their role in the process, from mediators to those providing support. This clarity prevents confusion and ensures accountability, keeping everyone aligned with the framework's objectives. Setting timelines and milestones is equally important. These guideposts provide a roadmap for progress, keeping the team focused and motivated. By breaking the resolution process into manageable phases, you can track progress and make necessary adjustments along the way. This structured approach helps facilitate smooth implementation and builds momentum toward a successful resolution.

As you begin implementing the framework, be prepared to face potential challenges. Resistance to change is a common obstacle, often rooted in fear of the unknown or discomfort with new processes. To overcome this, fostering an environment of open discussion and support is key. Encourage team members to voice their concerns and actively address them. Transparency in the process can alleviate fears and build trust. Miscommunication among stakeholders is another hurdle that can derail progress. Maintaining clarity and consistency in communication is critical to guarantee alignment among all team members.

Regular updates among team members can help prevent misunderstandings and keep the process moving forward. By anticipating these challenges and proactively addressing them, you can navigate the implementation process more effectively. Progress check-ins also provide an opportunity to assess the framework's effectiveness and make necessary adjustments. These meetings allow you to address any issues early on, preventing them from escalating into larger problems. Feedback loops are valuable for continuous improvement. Encourage team members to provide feedback on the process, identifying areas for refinement. This feedback can inform future iterations of the framework. By incorporating these strategies, you create a dynamic and responsive conflict resolution process that can adapt to changing needs and circumstances.

Consider this case study: a multinational corporation facing a cross-departmental conflict. The company implemented a step-by-step resolution framework, starting with assigning roles to key stakeholders. Each department head was responsible for facilitating communication and collaboration within their teams. Timelines and milestones were established, with regular check-ins to assess progress. Despite initial resistance, open communication and transparency helped build trust among team members. Feedback loops allowed for continuous improvement, with adjustments made based on input from all parties involved. As a result, the conflict was resolved, leading to improved collaboration and increased productivity across departments.

This example illustrates the power of a well-executed conflict resolution framework. By assigning clear roles, setting timelines, and fostering open communication, the corporation was able to navigate challenges and achieve a successful resolution. The continuous improvement process ensured the framework's adaptability, making it a valuable tool for future conflicts. This approach not only resolved the immediate issue, but also strengthened the organization's ability to manage conflicts proactively.

As you implement your own framework, remember that it's crucial to maintain adaptability and attentiveness to your team's evolving needs, guaranteeing the approach's efficacy and longevity. To effectively evaluate the outcomes of conflict resolution strategies, employing both qualitative and quantitative methods is essential. Utilizing anonymous surveys and feedback from participants provides direct insight into the satisfaction level and areas needing improvement. Moreover, analyzing conflict recurrence rates offers a quantifiable measure of strategy success. A decrease in recurring conflicts signifies effective resolution, whereas an increase indicates areas requiring further attention. By leveraging these tools, managers can achieve a comprehensive understanding of strategy impacts and make informed decisions on necessary adaptations.

Each review is an opportunity for learning, adapting, and growing, enhancing the manager's and team's capabilities. This commitment to ongoing assessment and refinement fosters a dynamic and resilient conflict resolution framework capable of navigating modern workplace complexities, ultimately improving conflict management and team cohesion.

3.4 Ensuring Long-Term Conflict Resolution Success

Sustaining the momentum of conflict resolution efforts is a critical challenge faced by many organizations. It's not merely about resolving a single dispute; it's about embedding these practices into the very fabric of organizational culture. This means that conflict resolution should become second nature to everyone in the company. One effective strategy is to integrate conflict resolution skills into regular training programs, ensuring that both new hires and seasoned employees understand its importance. By making conflict management a core part of professional development, you instill a mindset that values proactive communication and collaborative problem-solving.

Monitoring the ongoing success of these efforts requires diligent tracking and analysis. Key performance indicators (KPIs) tailored for conflict resolution can offer valuable insights. These might include metrics such as the frequency of conflicts, the time taken to resolve them, or employee satisfaction before and after resolution efforts. Regular reporting and analysis of these KPIs help maintain focus on continuous improvement. By keeping a close eye on these indicators, you can spot trends and adapt strategies as needed, ensuring that conflict resolution efforts remain aligned with organizational goals. This systematic approach highlights areas for improvement and celebrates successes, reinforcing the value of conflict resolution within the company.

Leadership plays a pivotal role in sustaining these efforts. Leaders who commit to continuous improvement in conflict resolution set the tone for the entire organization. It's crucial for leaders to model the behavior they wish to see, demonstrating active engagement in resolution processes and supporting team members in developing their own conflict management skills. Leadership commitment should be visible and genuine, going beyond mere words to tangible actions that foster a culture of open communication and trust. When leaders prioritize conflict resolution, they empower employees to address issues constructively, leading to a more cohesive and resilient workforce.

A striking example of sustained success in conflict resolution can be seen in a tech company that made significant strides in improving employee satisfaction. Initially plagued by high turnover and frequent disputes, the company embarked on a comprehensive conflict resolution initiative. They focused on training leaders to handle conflicts effectively and encouraged open dialogue across all levels. Over time, these efforts paid off, resulting in a marked improvement in workplace morale and productivity. Employees felt valued and heard, leading to a more positive work environment where conflicts were seen as opportunities for growth rather than obstacles. This transformation was not instantaneous, but the result of a sustained commitment to integrating conflict resolution into the organization's DNA. By embedding these practices into their culture, the company resolved existing issues and built a foundation for enduring success.

3.5 Customizing Frameworks for Organizational Needs

Tailoring conflict resolution frameworks to fit the unique needs of your organization is not a luxury—it's a necessity. Every workplace has its own culture and values that influence how conflicts arise and are perceived. Understanding these nuances is key to developing strategies that resonate with your team. Customization enhances effectiveness because it acknowledges and respects the distinct identity of an organization, making conflict resolution more intuitive and less intrusive.

Different industries face unique conflict scenarios that require specialized frameworks. In healthcare, for example, conflicts might arise not just from interdepartmental issues, but also from patient care demands. Here, the stakes are high, and the repercussions of unresolved conflicts can be severe. Frameworks in such settings might incorporate protocols for patient safety and care standards, alongside traditional conflict resolution techniques. In contrast, a creative agency dealing with artistic differences might focus on collaboration and shared vision, integrating brainstorming sessions into their resolution process. Each industry presents its own set of challenges and opportunities, and frameworks should be adapted to reflect these realities. By tailoring strategies to industry-specific needs, managers can address conflicts more effectively, ensuring that resolutions are both practical and meaningful.

Customization, however, is not without its challenges. Striking a balance between standardization and flexibility can be tricky. Standardization offers consistency and clarity, which are crucial for fairness and accountability. Yet, too much rigidity can prevent the framework from addressing specific issues unique to the organization. The key lies in creating a flexible structure that allows for adjustments without losing its core principles. Also, by involving team members in the customization process, you can gather diverse perspectives that enrich the framework. This collaborative approach enhances the framework's relevance and fosters a sense of ownership and commitment among employees. When they see their input reflected in the resolution process, they are more likely to engage with and support its implementation.

An example of successful customization can be seen through the healthcare example discussed above, addressing conflicts unique to patient care environments. Faced with frequent disputes between clinical staff, the institution developed a tailored framework that integrated patient safety protocols with conflict resolution practices. This approach ensured that patient care remained the top priority while providing a structured process for resolving staff disagreements. The institution also incorporated training sessions focused on communication and empathy, recognizing the emotional demands placed on healthcare professionals. This customization not only resolved existing conflicts, but also improved overall team cohesion and enhanced patient outcomes. By aligning their framework with the specific needs and values of their organization, the institution created a sustainable model for managing conflicts in a high-stakes environment.

Incorporating customization into conflict resolution frameworks is a strategic move that recognizes the diversity and complexity of modern workplaces. It allows managers to address conflicts with precision and sensitivity, acknowledging the unique challenges faced by their teams. As you consider how to tailor your framework, keep in mind the importance of understanding your organization's culture, adapting to industry-specific needs, and balancing flexibility with standardization. By doing so, you can develop a conflict resolution strategy that is effective and will resonate with your team.

FOUR

Mediation and Negotiation Skills

E nvision an office buzzing with activity where two previously cooperative departments are now locked in a conflict over resource allocation. This standoff is causing visible strain and a decline in overall productivity. As a manager, you are tasked with the delicate role of mediator. This requires a keen understanding of human dynamics. Mediation, unlike arbitration where a decision is imposed, allows parties to reach a mutually agreeable solution through facilitated dialogue. The aim here is not merely to compromise, but to enable each individual to voice their concerns and collaboratively find a resolution.

4.1 Your Role as a Mediator

As a mediator, your role is to guide the conversation, ensuring that each party has the opportunity to voice their perspective while maintaining a focus on finding a solution. This requires active listening, thoughtful questioning, and the ability to summarize discussions effectively. As a quick refresher, active listening involves fully concentrating on what is being said rather than passively hearing the words. It's about understanding the emotions and intentions behind the words, which is crucial in defusing tensions. By asking open-ended questions, you encourage parties to elaborate on their viewpoints, uncovering underlying interests that may not be immediately apparent. This technique aids in gathering information and also in helping individuals feel heard and validated.

The mediation process begins with an initial assessment and preparation, where you gather all relevant information and set the stage for the discussion. This includes understanding the key issues, identifying the stakeholders involved, and establishing ground rules to ensure a respectful and productive dialogue. Once the groundwork is laid, you facilitate the conversation, guiding the parties through a series of discussions aimed at exploring their differences and identifying common ground. Throughout this process, your role is to remain impartial, focusing on the issues rather than the individuals. By summarizing key points and reflecting on what has been said, you help clarify misunderstandings and keep the conversation on track.

Consider this example of a manager who successfully mediated a workplace dispute. In this case, two team leaders were at odds over project priorities, each convinced that their approach was the best path forward. By employing mediation techniques, the manager created a safe space for open dialogue, allowing each leader to present their case without interruption. Through active listening and thoughtful questioning, the manager helped uncover shared goals that both leaders could rally behind. By focusing on these commonalities, they were able to devise a collaborative plan that satisfied both parties, ultimately enhancing team cohesion and project outcomes. This case illustrates the power of mediation in turning potential conflicts into opportunities for growth and collaboration.

The skills required for effective mediation are not innate but can be developed through practice and reflection. Reflective listening practices, where you paraphrase and mirror back what has been said, can significantly enhance your mediation capabilities. This shows empathy and understanding and helps clarify any ambiguities, ensuring that all parties are on the same page. By honing these skills, you can become a more effective mediator, capable of navigating complex interpersonal dynamics and fostering a more compatible workplace.

Interactive Exercise: Practicing Mediation Skills

To refine your mediation skills, we recommend a hands-on approach through role-playing exercises that mimic real workplace conflicts. Begin by partnering with a peer to enact a specific scenario where two parties are at an impasse. You and your colleague will alternate roles, each taking a turn as the mediator.

In this controlled environment, concentrate on genuinely understanding the perspectives of both sides, rather than simply waiting for your turn to speak. Use open-ended questions to delve into the core of the conflict, helping both parties to articulate their needs and concerns more clearly. This could include questions like, "What outcome would you consider fair?" or "Can you elaborate on why this issue is important to you?"

After the exercise, take time to debrief with your partner. Discuss what strategies you found effective and pinpoint areas where you felt challenged or where the conversation could have veered off course. This reflective process is crucial for converting theory into practice, allowing you to identify personal strengths and areas for growth in your mediation approach. This practical exercise not only sharpens your mediation skills, but also builds confidence in your ability to navigate and defuse conflicts constructively. By regularly engaging in these simulations, you'll enhance your competency in guiding real-world disputes toward resolution.

4.2 The Role of Neutrality in Mediation

In the intricate dance of mediation, neutrality acts as the anchor that holds the process steady. It's more than just a principle; it's the foundation upon which trust and credibility are built. Picture yourself as a mediator in a dispute where emotions are high and each party feels equally justified in their stance. Your ability to remain impartial, like a calm harbor in a storm, ensures that both sides feel heard and respected. When parties sense even a hint of bias, the entire process is jeopardized. They may perceive the mediator as an ally of the opposing side, leading to disengagement and mistrust. The risk of perceived bias can derail attempts at resolution, making neutrality not just beneficial, but crucial.

Maintaining neutrality requires deliberate effort and a clear strategy. One effective approach is to avoid language that suggests favoritism. Neutral language helps set the tone for a fair and unbiased dialogue. For example, instead of saying, "I think you should consider...", opt for, "Let's explore some options together." This subtle shift in wording places the focus on collaboration rather than directive, ensuring that your language remains even-handed. Keeping personal opinions out of discussions is equally important. It's natural to have personal thoughts about the conflict, but expressing them can undermine your neutrality. Strive to be a conduit for dialogue rather than a participant in the debate. By refraining from sharing personal beliefs, you reinforce your role as an impartial facilitator, dedicated to guiding the parties towards their own resolution.

However, it's challenging to remain neutral in all instances. Accusations of bias can arise, whether grounded in reality or perception. If this happens, it's vital to address any claims head-on with transparency and openness. Reaffirm your commitment to impartiality and invite feedback on how you can better support the process. This reassures the parties involved and demonstrates your dedication to a fair resolution. Additionally, consider enlisting the help of a co-mediator if you feel your neutrality might be compromised. Having another neutral party can lend balance to the process and mitigate any perceptions of bias. By being proactive and transparent, you can overcome the challenges of maintaining neutrality and steer the mediation towards a successful outcome.

The benefits of a neutral mediation approach are profound. When parties trust in the mediator's impartiality, they are more willing to engage openly in the resolution process. This trust creates a safe space for honest communication, allowing parties to explore their differences without fear of judgment or reprisal. It empowers parties to take ownership of the outcome, fostering a sense of collaboration and mutual respect. This empowerment enhances the likelihood of reaching an agreement and strengthens relationships, turning what could have been a divisive conflict into an opportunity for growth and understanding. Neutrality, therefore, is not merely a tool for resolving disputes; it is a catalyst for creating productive and harmonious work environments.

4.3 Effective Negotiation Tactics

Negotiation is an intricate dance, where understanding the difference between interests and positions can make all the difference. A position represents the explicit demand or outcome that one party wants, whereas the underlying interest is the true motivation behind this demand—the fundamental need or desire prompting it. Imagine two departments vying for a limited budget. One insists on funding for a new project, while the other demands resources for ongoing operations. On the surface, these positions seem at odds, but delving deeper reveals shared interests in optimizing productivity and enhancing team morale. Recognizing these interests allows for creative solutions that satisfy both parties, rather than getting stuck on rigid positions.

A robust toolkit of negotiation tactics can empower you to navigate these complex scenarios with confidence. One tool is the concept of BATNA, or Best Alternative to a Negotiated Agreement. This involves understanding your fallback options should negotiations fail. By knowing your BATNA, you gain leverage, as you're aware of the minimum acceptable outcome. For instance, if negotiating a supplier contract, your BATNA might be an alternative vendor offering similar terms. This knowledge strengthens your position and informs your strategy, enabling more confident decision-making. Anchoring techniques are another powerful tactic. This involves setting the initial terms of negotiation to frame the discussion. By establishing the first offer, you create a reference point that can influence the course of negotiations. Anchoring is particularly effective when backed by well-researched justifications, making your terms appear reasonable and well-founded.

This requires preparation before negotiating. It involves a thorough understanding of both your position and that of the opposing party. Begin by gathering relevant information and data, ensuring you're well-versed in all aspects of the negotiation. This might include market research, historical precedents, or performance metrics. Armed with this knowledge, you can anticipate counterarguments and tailor your strategy accordingly. Setting clear objectives and limits is equally crucial. Define what you aim to achieve and the boundaries beyond which you won't compromise. This clarity guides your actions and prevents concessions that could undermine your interests. With well-defined goals and limits, you can navigate negotiations with precision and purpose.

Consider a scenario where strategic anchoring secured a beneficial agreement. A tech company was negotiating a merger, with both parties initially focused on maximizing their respective valuations. By employing anchoring techniques, one party set the tone by proposing a valuation based on future growth potential rather than current earnings. This approach reframed the discussion, aligning both parties on a shared vision for growth. As negotiations progressed, they were able to craft a deal that recognized this potential, resulting in a merger that benefited both sides. This example illustrates how anchoring, when combined with a clear understanding of interests and thorough preparation, can lead to favorable outcomes.

Negotiation is a multifaceted skill that requires a blend of strategy, empathy, and adaptability. By focusing on interests rather than positions, employing a diverse range of tactics, and committing to meticulous preparation, you can enhance your negotiation effectiveness. This approach not only increases the likelihood of achieving your desired outcomes, but also fosters positive, collaborative relationships with negotiating partners. As you refine your skills, you'll find that negotiation becomes less of a battlefield and more of a cooperative endeavor, where both parties can emerge satisfied and stronger.

4.4 Finding Win-Win Solutions

In the competitive landscape of business, the notion of win-win negotiation stands out as a beacon of collaboration. This approach focuses on creating agreements that satisfy the needs of all parties involved, leading to sustainable and mutually beneficial outcomes. At its core, win-win negotiation is about moving away from the mindset of winners and losers. Instead, it embraces collaboration, where both sides work together to expand the pie rather than fight over its pieces. By prioritizing mutual gains, you lay the foundation for agreements that resolve immediate issues and build long-term partnerships. This collaborative approach fosters goodwill and trust, essential components in maintaining positive relationships.

Identifying win-win opportunities requires a keen eye for shared interests and values. One effective method is to conduct brainstorming sessions that encourage creative problem-solving. These sessions should focus on identifying common goals and exploring various solutions that address the needs of all parties. By fostering an environment where ideas can flow freely, you open the door to innovative solutions that might not have been considered otherwise. Another strategy is to delve into the underlying values and interests of each party. Understanding what truly matters to each side allows you to craft solutions that resonate on a deeper level, ensuring that each party feels their core needs are met.

Despite its many advantages, achieving win-win outcomes is no easy feat. One significant barrier is the zero-sum mindset, where parties view negotiation as a competition rather than a collaboration. This mindset can lead to rigid positions and an unwillingness to explore alternative solutions. Overcoming this requires a shift in perspective, where the focus is on collaboration rather than competition. Encouraging open communication and transparency can help break down these barriers, paving the way for more cooperative discussions. Another challenge is the additional time and energy required to reach a win-win solution. While the process may be more involved, the long-term benefits of a mutually satisfying agreement far outweigh the initial investment.

Consider this scenario, where two companies entered a partnership agreement that enhanced both their market reaches. Initially, they were at odds over resources and branding. However, by focusing on shared interests, such as expanding customer bases and increasing revenue, they were able to identify synergies that benefited both sides. Through collaborative brainstorming, they devised a joint marketing strategy that leveraged each company's strengths. This approach not only resolved the immediate conflict, but also laid the groundwork for a successful partnership that exceeded their individual capacities. This case study illustrates how win-win negotiation can transform potential conflicts into opportunities for growth and collaboration, ultimately leading to outcomes that are greater than the sum of their parts.

The path to finding win-win solutions is paved with collaboration, creativity, and a willingness to explore new possibilities. As you engage in negotiations, remember that the goal is not just to reach an agreement, but to build relationships that foster long-term success. By focusing on mutual gains and embracing a collaborative spirit, you can navigate even the most complex negotiations with confidence and poise, ensuring that all parties leave the table satisfied and empowered.

4.5 Managing Power Dynamics in Negotiation

In any negotiation, power dynamics play a crucial role in shaping the outcome. They are the invisible threads that can either bind or unravel the fabric of discussions. Power imbalances can skew negotiations, allowing one party to dominate, while leaving the other feeling disenfranchised. Picture this, where a small supplier negotiates terms with a large corporation. The corporation, with its vast resources and market influence, holds significant leverage, potentially dictating terms that serve its interests while sidelining the supplier's needs. Recognizing these power plays is essential for navigating negotiations successfully. As a manager, understanding where the leverage points lie allows you to address imbalances, creating a more equitable environment.

To manage these dynamics effectively, establishing ground rules for fairness is vital. These rules act as the framework within which all parties operate, ensuring that the negotiation remains balanced and just. Clearly defined rules might include equal speaking time or the use of a neutral third-party facilitator to guide discussions. These measures prevent dominant parties from overshadowing others, fostering an environment where all voices can be heard. Empowering disadvantaged parties to voice their needs is another critical strategy. Encourage open dialogue by creating a safe space for expression, where individuals feel comfortable sharing their perspectives without fear of retribution. This empowerment balances the scales and enriches the negotiation by introducing diverse viewpoints that might have gone unheard otherwise.

Transparency is a powerful tool in mitigating power imbalances. By sharing information equitably, you level the playing field, allowing all parties to negotiate from an informed position. Imagine a labor negotiation where management holds all the data on company finances, while employees are left in the dark. This asymmetry can lead to mistrust and resentment, undermining any potential agreement. Instead, by openly sharing relevant information, management demonstrates goodwill, building trust and encouraging collaboration. Transparency fosters an atmosphere of honesty and openness, where parties are more likely to engage in constructive dialogue, paving the way for equitable outcomes.

Navigating power dynamics requires a nuanced understanding of the forces at play and a commitment to fairness and transparency. It demands a willingness to address imbalances head-on, creating an environment where there is mutual respect. By establishing ground rules, empowering voices, and promoting transparency, you can manage power dynamics effectively, transforming potential conflicts into opportunities for collaboration and growth. In doing so, negotiations become not just a means to an end, but a process that builds stronger relationships.

4.6 Closing the Deal: Ensuring Agreement Compliance

Securing commitment to agreements is the final, yet crucial, step in the negotiation process. Without ensuring compliance, even the most meticulously crafted agreement can fall apart, unraveling the hard-earned progress made by all parties involved. The importance of follow-through cannot be overstated. It is the glue that holds the resolution together, fostering trust and strengthening relationships. When parties see that commitments are honored, trust is built, and this trust is the cornerstone of any successful, long-lasting relationship. Conversely, when promises are broken, it can lead to a breakdown in trust, making future negotiations more challenging and fraught with skepticism.

To ensure compliance, it is important to have clear documentation of the terms and responsibilities. Every agreement should be detailed in a written format, outlining the obligations and expectations of each party. This serves as a reference point that can be revisited if disputes arise, ensuring that there is no ambiguity about what was decided. Establishing timelines and checkpoints is another effective strategy. By setting specific milestones for when certain tasks or actions should be completed, you create a roadmap that guides the implementation of the agreement. These checkpoints provide opportunities to assess progress, address any issues early on, and make necessary adjustments to keep the process on track.

Monitoring and evaluation play a critical role in maintaining accountability. Regular progress reviews should be conducted to ensure that all parties are meeting their commitments. These reviews offer a platform to discuss any challenges or changes in circumstances that might affect the agreement, facilitating open communication and adaptation. By maintaining continuous over-sight, you ensure that the terms are being followed and further demonstrate a commitment to the agreement's success. This ongoing engagement fosters a collaborative spirit, where all parties feel invested in achieving the desired outcomes. With this approach, you can transform a negotiated agreement into a lasting and mutually beneficial relationship.

Add Your Thoughts to the Conversation on Conflict Management

We've been exploring the pivotal role of conflict resolution skills in effective management and how these skills—such as clear communication, emotional intelligence, structured frameworks, and mediation techniques—are essential in today's dynamic and fast-paced workplace. The modern organizational landscape brings both challenges and opportunities for resolving conflict, reshaping how managers lead, collaborate, and foster a harmonious work environment.

Building conflict resolution skills isn't about achieving perfection and eliminating all disagreements. It's about equipping managers with the tools to navigate complex interpersonal dynamics, understand diverse perspectives, and foster resilience in their teams to overcome these challenges and setbacks.

At this point in your reading, I hope you've recognized how the strategies outlined in this book can lead to positive outcomes, such as enhanced team cohesion, improved productivity, and a more supportive workplace culture. If the insights and techniques in this book have made a meaningful impact on your approach to conflict resolution, you're in a great position to share these benefits with other managers and leaders.

By leaving a review on Amazon, you'll help others discover practical tools to address workplace conflicts effectively and strengthen their management skills.

Share your thoughts on this book and your own experiences applying its strategies. One of the most powerful ways to reinforce your learning is by helping others understand and apply these concepts.

Please scan the QR code to leave a review.

Thank you for your support. Together, we can demonstrate the transformative power of mastering conflict resolution skills in creating thriving, collaborative workplaces.

FIVE

Building a Conflict-Positive Culture

I magine a bustling startup where creativity flows as freely as the coffee in the break room. Yet, beneath the surface, minor tensions brew among team members, threatening to disrupt the harmony. As a manager, you recognize that these conflicts could stifle innovation and productivity if they are not addressed. The challenge lies in transforming these tensions into opportunities for growth, fostering an environment where conflict is not feared but embraced as a catalyst for positive change. This chapter explores how to cultivate a culture that views conflict as a constructive force, beginning with the cornerstone of open dialogue.

5.1 Enabling Open Dialogue

Open dialogue is crucial for effective conflict resolution. When communication channels remain open, conflicts can be addressed swiftly and constructively, preventing them from festering into larger issues. Regular team check-ins serve as the foundation for this openness, providing a structured space where team members can share updates, concerns, and ideas. These meetings, whether weekly or biweekly, create a continuous cadence of communication that keeps everyone aligned and aware of each other's challenges and achievements. Additionally, creating forums for anonymous feedback can further enhance this openness. By allowing team members to voice concerns without fear of reprisal, you encourage candidness and honesty, leading to a more transparent and cohesive team environment. These forums can be as simple as suggestion boxes or digital platforms where employees can share their thoughts discreetly.

Fostering an environment of constructive criticism requires deliberate strategies that encourage honest and respectful feedback. One effective method is the "feedback sandwich," a technique that frames criticism between positive observations. This approach softens the delivery of critical feedback and reinforces the recipient's strengths, making the feedback more palatable and actionable. Training sessions focused on giving and receiving feedback can further support this environment. These sessions equip team members with the skills to articulate their thoughts clearly and respectfully, whether delivering praise or constructive criticism. By normalizing feedback as a tool for growth rather than judgment, you cultivate a culture where continuous improvement is embraced.

Despite the benefits, maintaining open dialogue presents challenges. Fear of retribution or misunderstandings can suppress communication, leading team members to withhold their true thoughts and feelings. Building trust within your team is essential to overcoming these barriers. Trust is nurtured through consistency and transparency, demonstrating that open dialogue is valued and respected. When team members feel confident that their voices will be heard without negative repercussions, they are more likely to engage openly and honestly. Encouraging vulnerability and empathy within the team can also strengthen this trust.

By modeling vulnerability yourself—admitting mistakes, sharing your own learning experiences—you create a safe space for others to do the same.

Successful organizations have embraced open dialogue as a core component of their culture. Consider a tech company that regularly holds town hall meetings to address team concerns and gather feedback. In these meetings, leaders share updates on company progress and future plans, providing transparency and context for the team's work. They also open the floor to questions and suggestions, encouraging all employees to contribute their perspectives. This practice keeps the team informed, while also fostering a sense of ownership and involvement in the company's direction. As a result, employees feel more connected and engaged, leading to improved conflict outcomes. By adopting similar practices, you can create a culture where open dialogue is the norm, empowering your team to navigate conflicts with confidence and creativity.

Reflection Section: Open Dialogue Practices

Reflect on your current practices for fostering open dialogue within your team. Consider the following questions:

- How often do your team members have opportunities to share feedback openly?
- Are there mechanisms in place for anonymous feedback?
- What steps can you take to build trust and encourage vulnerability within your team?

Use these reflections to identify areas for improvement and develop strategies to enhance communication and openness in your team dynamic.

5.2 Strategies for Creating a Safe Conflict Space

Creating a safe space for conflict is about more than just physical surroundings; it's about fostering an environment where individuals feel secure to express their thoughts and concerns. This means cultivating both physical and psychological safety in the workplace. Physically, this could involve arranging comfortable meeting areas where team members can sit face-to-face in a neutral environment, free from distractions and power dynamics that might occur in someone's personal office. Psychologically, it involves nurturing a culture of respect and openness, where team members are encouraged to share their perspectives and listen to others with empathy. When team members feel safe, they are more likely to engage openly and honestly, which is vital for resolving conflicts effectively.

To create such a space, start by setting clear ground rules for respectful interaction. These rules should be developed collaboratively, ensuring that everyone has a say in what they entail. Typical guidelines might include listening without interrupting, refraining from personal attacks, and focusing on the issue rather than the individual. Establishing these norms helps to set the tone for discussions, making it clear that while differing opinions are welcome, disrespect is not. Another practical step is to designate neutral meeting areas for conflict discussions. These should be spaces that are comfortable and free from hierarchical implications. If unavailable, consider using virtual meeting platforms that allow participants to feel on equal footing, regardless of their physical location. Just make sure the cameras are on.

The benefits of a safe conflict space extend far beyond the meeting room. When team members feel secure, they are more inclined to participate in conflict resolution processes, leading to more robust and creative solutions. This increased willingness to engage often results in more productive discussions, as individuals feel free to share ideas and challenge assumptions without fearing negative repercussions. Furthermore, a safe space encourages a sense of ownership and accountability, as team members recognize that their contributions are valued and respected. This can lead to a more cohesive team dynamic, where conflicts are seen as opportunities for growth and innovation rather than obstacles to be avoided.

Maintaining this safety over time requires consistent effort and vigilance. Regular safety audits and feedback sessions can help ensure that the environment remains supportive and inclusive. These audits might involve anonymous surveys or one-on-one conversations to gauge how safe team members feel in conflict situations. Feedback gathered from these sessions can then inform any necessary adjustments to the ground rules or meeting practices. It's also important to continually reinforce the value of a safe conflict space through leadership actions and organizational policies. Leaders should model the behaviors they wish to see, demonstrating respect, empathy, and a willingness to listen. By consistently prioritizing safety, you can create a workplace culture where conflict is approached constructively, fostering innovation and collaboration.

Interactive Element: Safe Space Assessment

Consider conducting a "Safe Space Assessment" within your team. Invite team members to anonymously share their thoughts on how safe they feel during conflict discussions. Ask for specific examples of what contributes to their sense of safety or, conversely, what detracts from it. Use this feedback to identify strengths and areas for improvement, adjusting ground rules and meeting practices as necessary. This ongoing dialogue enhances the safety of your conflict space and empowers team members to take an active role in shaping the environment in which they work.

5.3 Conflict as a Catalyst for Innovation

Conflict and innovation might seem like unlikely companions, yet history shows us that disagreements can fuel groundbreaking ideas. Consider the invention of the airplane. The Wright brothers, driven by the challenge of human flight, faced intense skepticism and internal debates. Yet, their persistence through conflict led to a revolutionary breakthrough. Similarly, the creation of the Internet was fraught with technical disagreements, yet these conflicts pushed engineers to develop the robust systems we rely on today. In the workplace, conflict can ignite creative problem-solving. When managed correctly, it transforms tension into a platform for exploring diverse perspectives and solutions.

Leveraging conflict for creative problem-solving requires intentional strategies. One effective method is incorporating brainstorming sessions into conflict resolution meetings. These sessions should encourage all team members to voice ideas, no matter how unconventional they might seem. By fostering an environment where every suggestion is valued, you open the door to innovative solutions that might not have emerged in a more controlled setting. Diverse teams bring unique viewpoints, and when these differences clash, they can lead to creative friction. If directed constructively, this friction can result in solutions that are more comprehensive and innovative than those conceived in homogenous groups.

Changing the cultural mindset to view conflict positively involves a shift from seeing it as a disruptive force to recognizing its potential for growth. Organizations that have successfully embraced conflict-driven innovation illustrate this cultural transformation.

For example, a tech company known for its cutting-edge products attributes much of its success to its approach to conflict. Rather than stifling disagreements, it encourages open debates during development phases, viewing them as opportunities to test and refine ideas. This approach leads to better products and nurtures a culture of continuous improvement and collaboration. Employees learn to view disagreements not as personal attacks, but as critical evaluations meant to enhance their work.

This real-world scenario further demonstrates how conflict can lead to significant innovations. Take a marketing team that was struggling with a declining product line. A heated debate ensued over the direction of a new campaign. Ideas clashed, but through this conflict, a novel approach emerged. The team decided to pivot their strategy entirely, launching a campaign that tapped into an overlooked market segment. The result was a resounding success, revitalizing the product line and setting a new standard for future campaigns. This example shows how conflict, when approached with an open mind and strategic intent, can unlock new pathways to success.

To harness the potential of conflict, managers must cultivate an environment where it is safe to disagree and where diverse opinions are not just tolerated but actively sought. This involves training teams to engage constructively, focusing on ideas rather than personalities. By promoting a mindset that views conflict as a natural and beneficial part of the creative process, you can transform your team's approach to challenges. Encourage team members to bring their unique perspectives to the table, and facilitate discussions that explore the full spectrum of possibilities. In doing so, you drive innovation and build a resilient team prepared to tackle future challenges with creativity and confidence.

5.4 Training Teams for Conflict Competence

Conflict competence enables teams to address disagreements constructively, reducing tension and fostering a collaborative spirit. When team members are equipped with the skills to handle disputes, the workplace transforms into a space where differences are managed, not feared. This competence reduces workplace tension significantly, as team members learn to view conflict not as a threat but as an opportunity for dialogue and growth. It shifts the focus from avoiding disagreements to addressing them head-on, encouraging a culture of openness and resilience where challenges are met with confidence and creativity.

Developing a comprehensive training program for conflict competence requires a well-structured framework, one that encompasses the core skills needed to manage conflicts effectively. A robust program should include modules on communication, negotiation, and emotional intelligence. Communication training focuses on active listening, clear expression, and understanding non-verbal cues. Negotiation skills are crucial for finding mutually beneficial solutions, teaching team members how to balance assertiveness with empathy. Emotional intelligence training helps individuals recognize and manage their emotions and those of others, promoting empathy and reducing misunderstandings. Interactive workshops and role-playing exercises are essential components of this training too. They provide a safe environment for team members to practice and refine their conflict resolution skills, allowing them to experiment with different approaches and receive feedback in real-time. By simulating real-life scenarios, these exercises build confidence and prepare team members to apply their skills effectively in actual situations.

There are several benefits to investing in conflict competence training, that could be leveraged if you need buy in and financial support from leadership. Teams that undergo these training handle conflicts more effectively and efficiently, leading to increased collaboration and reduced resolution times. With enhanced skills, team members can address issues promptly, preventing them from escalating into larger disputes. This proactive approach saves time and strengthens team cohesion, as individuals learn to work through their differences and find common ground. Trained teams are better equipped to navigate the complexities of modern work environments, where diverse perspectives and high-pressure situations are common. They develop the resilience needed to thrive in such settings, turning potential conflicts into opportunities for growth and innovation.

Consider the example from earlier, of a healthcare team that significantly reduced patient care conflicts through targeted training. Initially, the team faced frequent disagreements over treatment plans, which affected patient outcomes and team morale. By implementing a conflict competence training program, the team learned to communicate more effectively and collaborate more closely. The training included role-playing exercises that mirrored common patient care scenarios, allowing team members to practice their skills in a controlled environment. As a result, the team became more adept at resolving conflicts quickly and amicably, leading to improved patient satisfaction and increased team morale. This success story illustrates the transformative power of conflict competence training. By investing in the development of these skills, organizations can foster a culture of collaboration and innovation.

Training for conflict competence is not just about equipping individuals with new skills; it's about embedding these skills into the team's daily practices and culture. It requires ongoing commitment and reinforcement, ensuring that the skills are continually honed and applied. Regular refresher workshops and feedback sessions can help sustain the momentum, keeping the team engaged and motivated. By prioritizing conflict competence, managers can create a work environment where differences are celebrated, and conflicts are approached with grace. This commitment to conflict competence training empowers teams to navigate challenges effectively, turning potential obstacles into stepping stones for success.

5.5 Leadership's Role in Cultivating a Positive Culture

In any organization, the tone of the workplace culture is set from the top. Leaders play a crucial role in shaping an environment where conflict is not seen as a threat but as an opportunity for growth. By leading by example, leaders demonstrate how conflicts should be approached and resolved, setting a precedent for the entire team to follow. When leaders handle conflicts with transparency and integrity, they show that open dialogue and constructive criticism are valued. This approach helps establish a norm where employees feel safe to express their concerns and ideas, knowing that their perspectives will be respected and considered. The behavior of leaders sends a powerful message about what is acceptable and expected, influencing the overall atmosphere and dynamics of the workplace.

Promoting a positive culture requires intentional actions from leaders. One effective strategy is to implement regular team-building activities that foster a sense of camaraderie and trust among team members. These activities can range from informal social gatherings to structured workshops focused on collaboration and problem-solving. By bringing the team together in a relaxed setting, leaders can break down barriers and encourage open communication. Recognizing and rewarding constructive conflict management is another crucial step. We will expand on this one in the next section (5.6), so hold this thought.

Despite the benefits, cultivating a positive culture has its challenges. Resistance to cultural change is a common obstacle that leaders must navigate. Employees may be accustomed to a certain way of doing things and may resist efforts to shift the culture. Overcoming this resistance requires patience and persistence. Leaders need to communicate the benefits of a positive culture clearly and consistently, addressing any concerns or misconceptions that may arise. Providing training and support can also help ease the transition, equipping employees with the skills and confidence needed to embrace new ways of working. Additionally, leaders must be willing to adapt their own behaviors and strategies as needed, demonstrating a commitment to continuous improvement and learning. By modeling flexibility and openness to change, leaders can inspire their teams to do the same.

There are numerous examples of leaders who have successfully fostered positive cultures within their organizations. One notable case is a CEO who transformed a company's approach to conflict through transparent communication. Faced with high employee turnover and low morale, the CEO recognized the need for change. By implementing a series of town hall meetings and open forums, the CEO encouraged employees to voice their concerns and share their ideas for improvement. This transparent approach helped identify the root causes of dissatisfaction and empowered employees to take an active role in shaping the company's future. The result was a more engaged and motivated workforce, with lower turnover rates and increased productivity. This example illustrates the transformative power of leadership in cultivating a positive culture.

As a leader, your actions set the tone for your organization's culture. By fostering a conflict-positive environment, you empower your team to embrace challenges and work together effectively. Through intentional actions and a commitment to open communication, you can create a workplace where differences are celebrated and conflicts are approached with positivity.

5.6 Celebrating Conflict Resolution Successes

Recognizing and celebrating successful conflict resolution can be a powerful tool to boost morale and motivation, cultivating a positive company culture. When employees see that their efforts to engage in respectful conflict resolution are acknowledged and appreciated, they are more likely to continue these practices. By celebrating these behaviors, leaders reinforce the importance of a conflict-positive culture and motivate others to follow suit.

Celebrating these successes can be done in creative and impactful ways. One effective method is implementing a 'Resolution of the Month' award. This award can highlight a team or individual who has demonstrated exceptional skills in managing a conflict constructively. Public recognition during team meetings or through internal communications can inspire others to strive for similar achievements. Sharing success stories in company newsletters offers another avenue for celebration. By detailing the challenges faced and the innovative solutions devised, these stories serve as inspiration and education for the entire organization. They provide concrete examples of conflict resolution in action, offering insights and strategies that others can learn from and emulate.

The impact of celebrating conflict resolution goes beyond immediate recognition. It fosters a culture of continuous commitment to resolving conflicts constructively, enhancing overall team dynamics. When employees see their efforts acknowledged, they become more engaged and willing to participate in future resolution efforts. This increased engagement translates into a proactive approach to conflict management, where team members are more likely to address issues before they escalate. Over time, this proactive mindset becomes ingrained in the organizational culture, leading to a more resilient and adaptable team. This shift improves the workplace environment and enhances the organization's capacity to innovate and grow.

Organizations that celebrate conflict successes often see significant benefits to their culture. For example, a startup known for its dynamic and collaborative environment hosts an annual 'Resolution Day' to honor team achievements in conflict management. On this day, teams come together to share their experiences, discuss challenges, and celebrate their resolutions. This event strengthens team bonds and reinforces the organization's commitment to open communication and collaboration. By creating a space for reflection and celebration, the startup cultivates a culture where conflicts are viewed as opportunities for growth and learning. This practice has contributed to the company's success, as employees feel empowered to tackle challenges head-on, knowing their efforts will be recognized and celebrated.

The practice of celebrating conflict resolution can transform how teams perceive and engage with conflicts. It shifts the narrative from one of avoidance and aversion to one of opportunity and growth. This cultural shift improves team dynamics and enhances overall organizational performance. As employees become more skilled and confident in their conflict resolution abilities, they contribute to a more harmonious and innovative workplace. This transformation is not instantaneous, but through consistent recognition and celebration, it becomes an integral part of the organizational fabric, paving the way for sustained success and growth.

SIX

Dealing with Difficult Personalities

I n the vibrant ecosystem of the modern workplace, a melting pot of personalities is inevitable. Envision an office where collaboration is key, yet beneath the surface there are personality conflicts brewing. This scenario is all too common: the harshness of one team member grating against another's sensitivity, breeding a climate of discomfort. These differences can significantly impact team dynamics, leading to reduced productivity and morale. Understanding and identifying difficult personality types becomes crucial for maintaining harmony and fostering a thriving environment.

6.1 Defining Personality Types

Personality conflicts often stem from the diverse ways individuals express themselves and interact with others. While diversity enriches team perspectives, it can also lead to misunderstandings and friction. Recognizing and addressing these conflicts requires a keen understanding of the different personality types that populate the workplace. Tools like the Myers-Briggs Type Indicator

(MBTI) offer valuable insights into personality traits, helping managers better navigate interpersonal dynamics. By understanding each team member's communication preferences and behavioral tendencies, managers can tailor their approach, ensuring more effective interactions and reducing the potential for conflict.

To identify difficult personalities, managers can use observational techniques alongside personality assessments. Observing how individuals react under stress, how they communicate, and how they handle feedback provides valuable clues about their personality type. For instance, an aggressive personality may exhibit confrontational and domineering behaviors, often interrupting others and dismissing opposing views. These individuals typically thrive in competitive environments but can create tension within collaborative settings. On the other hand, passive-aggressive individuals may resist directly, using sarcasm or subtle defiance to express dissatisfaction. This indirect approach can lead to confusion and frustration among team members, as issues remain unresolved and simmer beneath the surface.

Narcissistic personalities present another unique challenge. Typically self-centered and lacking empathy, narcissists often struggle to accept criticism or responsibility. They demand admiration and can become manipulative to maintain their self-image. In the workplace, these individuals might dominate conversations, disregard others' contributions, or externalize blame. Their presence can disrupt team cohesion, as colleagues may feel undervalued or ignored. Understanding these traits allows managers to develop strategies to mitigate their impact, ensuring that team dynamics remain positive and productive.

Consider the case of a team member who consistently undermines others' contributions. This individual might take credit for colleagues' ideas or interrupt team discussions to assert their viewpoint. This behavior can erode trust and partnership, breeding resentment and disengagement. By identifying these patterns early, managers can intervene constructively, addressing the behavior and promoting a more inclusive culture. Recognizing these personality traits is the first step toward managing them effectively, reducing their potential to derail team progress.

Interactive Exercise: Personality Patterns Reflection

Take a moment to reflect on your team. Consider each member's unique personality traits and how they interact with others. Note any patterns or behaviors that stand out. Do certain individuals dominate meetings, or do others retreat when conflicts arise? Identifying these traits can help you tailor your management approach, ensuring more compatible team dynamics. This exercise encourages you to observe and understand your team, fostering a more empathetic and effective leadership style. Revisit this exercise biannually or annually to evaluate any observed changes or improvements in team dynamics and individual behaviors.

6.2 Strategies for Handling Aggressive Behaviors

Consider the impact of aggression on the workplace: it disrupts team harmony, lowers morale, and creates a hostile atmosphere. Imagine a team meeting where one member's aggressive tone silences others' contributions. This not only stifles creativity and collaboration but also instills a sense of fear and unease. Aggressive behavior can range from overt actions like shouting to subtler forms like dismissive comments or interruptions. The effects ripple through the team, eroding trust and damaging relationships. Addressing aggression is crucial to maintaining a healthy work environment. It requires a manager's steady hand to navigate these turbulent waters, ensuring conflicts do not spiral out of control.

One of the first steps in handling aggression is to remain calm and composed. This can be challenging, especially when faced with hostility, but it's vital. A composed demeanor helps defuse tension and sets a calm tone for the interaction. It signals to the aggressor that their behavior is unacceptable and won't be mirrored. Setting clear boundaries is equally important. By outlining acceptable behavior and enforcing limits, you emphasize respect and mutual understanding. When an aggressive colleague interrupts, firmly but respectfully state, "I'd like to finish my point." This not only reinforces boundaries, but also models assertive communication. De-escalation techniques, such as lowering your voice or using calm body language, can further diffuse aggressive situations. These strategies, when employed consistently, foster an environment where aggression is managed effectively.

Assertive communication is a powerful tool in addressing aggression. It involves expressing your feelings and needs clearly and respectfully, without resorting to aggression yourself. By using "I" statements, you can convey your perspective without assigning blame. For example, saying, "I feel frustrated when my contributions are interrupted," focuses on your experience rather than accusing the other person. This approach encourages openness and understanding, reducing defensiveness. Assertiveness demonstrates confidence and respect, qualities that can influence the workplace culture positively. By modeling assertive communication as a manager, you inspire others to adopt similar practices, gradually transforming the team's interaction dynamics.

This is yet another area where role-playing exercises can be invaluable for practicing these skills. By simulating confrontational meetings, managers can develop their ability to handle aggression in a controlled setting. Imagine a scenario where a team member aggressively disputes a project timeline. In a role-play, practice responding with calm assertiveness, maintaining eye contact, and using "I" statements to express your viewpoint. These exercises provide a safe space to experiment with different techniques and receive feedback on your approach. By refining your skills in these scenarios, you prepare yourself for real-world encounters, building confidence and competence in managing aggressive behaviors.

6.3 Managing Passive-Aggressiveness

Passive-aggressive behavior can be a silent disruptor. Unlike direct aggression, which is often overt, passive-aggressiveness lurks beneath the surface, undermining team cohesion and productivity. This behavior is characterized by indirect resistance and avoidance of direct communication, manifesting through actions such as procrastination, backhanded compliments, or the silent treatment. It's a confusing and frustrating dynamic that can erode trust and create an atmosphere of tension. When team members engage in passive-aggressive exchanges, the resulting ambiguity can lead to misunderstandings and a breakdown in collaboration. As a manager, it's crucial to recognize these behaviors early and address them head-on, ensuring that your team operates in a transparent and supportive environment.

Addressing passive-aggressive behavior requires a strategic approach that brings underlying issues to the forefront. Encouraging open and direct communication is a foundational step. Create an environment where team members feel safe to express their thoughts and feelings openly. This might involve setting aside dedicated time for one-on-one check-ins, where individuals can discuss their concerns without fear of judgment. During these conversations, emphasize the importance of honesty and clarity, and model these behaviors yourself. Additionally, when passive-aggressive behaviors arise, address them privately and constructively. Avoid public confrontations that can exacerbate the issue. Instead, invite the individual for a private discussion, focusing on specific behaviors and their impact on the team. This approach highlights the behavior, while opening the door for collaborative problem-solving.

Empathy plays a pivotal role in managing passive-aggressiveness. By understanding the root causes of this behavior, you can address the underlying insecurities or fears that drive it. Often, passive-aggressive individuals may feel powerless or undervalued, leading to indirect expressions of their discontent. Explore these emotions with empathy, seeking to understand their perspective and offering support. By validating their feelings and working together to find solutions, you can help them feel more secure and confident in their interactions. This empathetic approach fosters a culture of trust and openness, where team members are encouraged to communicate directly and honestly.

Consider a scenario where a manager successfully managed passive-aggressive behavior by fostering transparency and encouraging candid feedback. In this case, a team member frequently missed deadlines, offering vague excuses and deflecting blame onto others. Recognizing the pattern, the manager initiated a private conversation to explore the underlying issues. Through open dialogue, it became clear that the team member felt overwhelmed by their workload and uncertain about their role. By addressing these concerns and providing clear guidance and support, the manager was able to alleviate the individual's stress and encourage more direct communication. This intervention improved the team member's performance and strengthened the overall team dynamic, as others felt inspired to share their concerns openly.

6.4 Conflict Resolution with Narcissistic Individuals

Navigating conflicts with narcissistic individuals presents unique challenges due to their distinctive personality traits. These individuals often exhibit a strong need for admiration and a significant lack of empathy, which complicates conflict resolution. They find it challenging to accept criticism or responsibility, often deflecting blame onto others to maintain their self-image. This behavior can create a cycle of tension and frustration in the workplace, as colleagues may feel their concerns are dismissed or invalidated. The difficulty lies in the narcissist's perception of themselves as inherently superior, which can hinder constructive dialogue and mutual understanding. In a team setting, their self-centered approach can disrupt collaboration, leading to an environment where others might feel undervalued or unheard.

To effectively manage conflicts with narcissists, setting firm boundaries is critical. These boundaries must be consistent and clear, as they help define acceptable behavior and prevent manipulation. Establishing these limits provides a framework within which interactions can occur, reducing the potential for conflict escalation. It's important to communicate these boundaries assertively, ensuring that they are respected and enforced. Maintaining consistency in these interactions builds a stable environment where expectations are clear, minimizing opportunities for the narcissist to exploit any ambiguity. Additionally, focusing on facts rather than engaging in emotional arguments can prevent unnecessary power struggles. By steering conversations towards objective, data-driven discussions, you can bypass the narcissist's attempts to shift blame or evade responsibility.

Communication with narcissistic individuals requires careful navigation to avoid common pitfalls. Flattery and validation traps are tactics often employed by narcissists to manipulate situations to their advantage. While it might be tempting to use compliments to defuse tension, doing so can reinforce their behavior, leading to further challenges down the line. Instead, maintain a neutral tone and focus on the task at hand, emphasizing the importance of teamwork and shared goals. This approach redirects the conversation away from personal validation and towards collective success, aligning the narcissist's interests with the team's objectives.

Consider an example of a project lead who successfully managed a narcissistic team member by redirecting their focus towards team goals. This individual often sought recognition and dominated meetings, overshadowing others' contributions. By acknowledging their expertise in a specific area relevant to the project, the project lead was able to channel their energy into a collaborative effort. Encouraging the narcissist to take a leadership role in this context helped satisfy their need for acknowledgment while ensuring their efforts contributed to the team's success. This strategic redirection resolved the immediate conflict and fostered a more cooperative atmosphere, allowing other team members to engage more freely.

The process of resolving conflicts with narcissistic individuals requires patience and strategic thinking. It's about balancing the need to address issues directly while managing the individual's sensitivities. By establishing firm boundaries, focusing on objective discussions, and steering clear of validation traps, you can navigate these interactions more effectively. This approach mitigates potential conflicts and creates a more harmonious work environment, where all team members feel respected and valued, enabling them to contribute their best work.

6.5 Techniques for Bridging Personality Clashes

In any workplace, the tapestry of diverse personalities can be both a blessing and a curse. On one hand, diversity enriches team perspectives, offering a wide array of ideas and solutions. On the other, it can lead to misunderstandings and friction, particularly when differing personalities clash. Imagine a team where one member thrives on detailed planning while another prefers spontaneity. These differences, if unmanaged, can cause perpetual disagreements, slowing down progress. These types of situations can muddle communication, leading to a breakdown in team participation and a dip in team performance. Yet, when these differences are harnessed effectively, they can foster innovation and drive the team toward success. Managing these dynamics requires a thoughtful approach to bridge the gaps, ensuring that diversity becomes a strength rather than a source of division.

One effective technique for bridging personality differences is to organize team-building activities that highlight individual strengths. These activities not only foster camaraderie, but also allow team members to appreciate each other's unique contributions. By focusing on strengths, individuals learn to value what each person brings to the table, paving the way for more harmonious interactions. For instance, a brainstorming session where each member is encouraged to present ideas based on their strengths can illuminate the diverse talents within the team, fostering mutual respect and understanding. These activities serve as a reminder that while personalities may differ, everyone is working toward a shared goal.

Workshops on diversity and inclusion play an instrumental role in enhancing understanding and cooperation among team members. These workshops provide a structured environment where individuals can explore and discuss the nuances of different personality types, learning how to communicate more effectively across these differences. Through interactive exercises and open discussions, participants gain insights into their own biases and assumptions, equipping them with the tools to navigate complex interpersonal dynamics. By fostering a culture of inclusivity, these workshops help break down barriers, creating an environment where all voices are heard and valued. This understanding strengthens team cohesion and drives collective success by leveraging the full spectrum of team talents.

Creating shared goals is another powerful strategy for aligning diverse personalities. When team members rally around a common objective, it shifts the focus from individual differences to collective achievements. This alignment not only fosters collaboration but also reduces the likelihood of conflict, as everyone is working toward the same end. Setting clear, achievable goals encourages cooperation, as team members must communicate and coordinate to reach their objectives. This shared purpose serves as a unifying force, motivating individuals to set aside personal differences in favor of the greater good. As teams work together to achieve these goals, they develop a deeper appreciation for each other's strengths and capabilities, strengthening their overall performance.

Flexibility is crucial in managing personality clashes. This means adapting your communication style to suit different individuals, ensuring that your message resonates with each team member. For example, a detailed planner may appreciate a structured approach, while a big-picture thinker might respond better to broad concepts. By tailoring your communication to fit the audience, you can reduce misunderstandings and foster a more inclusive dialogue. Flexibility also extends to problem-solving, where being open to alternative perspectives can lead to innovative solutions. This adaptability not only eases tensions, but also creates a more dynamic and responsive team environment, where change is embraced and diversity is celebrated.

Consider the example of a cross-functional team that overcame personality differences by collaborating on shared projects. Initially, the team's varied approaches led to friction, with each member advocating for their own methods. However, by focusing on a common project goal, they learned to appreciate the unique perspectives each brought to the table. Through regular check-ins and open dialogue, they aligned their efforts, leveraging their differences to create a comprehensive and innovative solution. This successful integration enhanced the project outcome and strengthened team relationships, demonstrating the power of bridging personality clashes through shared purpose and mutual respect.

6.6 Building Alliances with Challenging Colleagues

In the workplace, building alliances can transform what might initially seem like adversarial relationships into collaborative partnerships. Challenging colleagues, often perceived as obstacles, can actually become valuable allies when approached strategically. By understanding their motivations and working styles, you unlock the potential to turn friction into synergy. This approach enhances team dynamics and leverages the unique strengths that these individuals bring to the table. By reframing these relationships, you shift the focus from conflict to collaboration, cultivating an environment where diverse ideas converge.

Developing trust and cooperation with difficult personalities requires deliberate effort and a thoughtful approach. Patience and persistence are also fundamental to building alliances with challenging colleagues. Relationships take time to evolve, and progress may be slow. It's important to remain patient, recognizing that change doesn't happen overnight. Be prepared for setbacks and misunderstandings, using them as learning opportunities rather than roadblocks. Persistence in maintaining the relationship, even when progress seems elusive, demonstrates your commitment to the alliance. Over time, this dedication can shift perceptions, transforming initial skepticism into cooperation. By consistently showing up and investing in the relationship, you lay the groundwork for a more cohesive work environment.

Consider this scenario where a manager successfully turned a challenging colleague into a project advocate. Initially, this colleague was resistant to change, often questioning new initiatives and pushing back against proposed strategies. Instead of viewing this resistance as a hindrance, the manager sought to understand the colleague's concerns and motivations. Through regular one-on-one meetings, they discovered shared interests in process improvement and efficiency. By aligning on these goals, the manager gradually won the colleague's support, transforming them into a key advocate for the project. This alliance improved project outcomes and strengthened team cohesion, as other team members witnessed the positive shift in dynamics. The colleague's insights and critical perspective proved invaluable, highlighting how alliances with challenging individuals can lead to unexpected and beneficial outcomes.

In navigating these relationships, it's crucial to approach interactions with openness and a willingness to learn. Challenging colleagues often offer unique perspectives that can enrich your understanding and approach to problem-solving. By embracing these differences and seeking common ground, you foster an environment where diverse ideas are valued and collaboration thrives. As you continue to build these relationships, you'll find that even the most challenging colleagues can become your strongest allies, driving success and growth for the entire team.

SEVEN

Legal and Ethical Considerations

I n a busy workplace where operations are smoothly progressing, an unexpected silence descends as rumors of a new policy begin to spread. A manager is called into human resources (HR) to discuss a complaint that hinges on the legal nuances of workplace interaction.

7.1 Legal Boundaries in Conflict Resolution

Understanding legal boundaries is crucial for managers to navigate the complex landscape of employment law and regulations. The intricate web of legal frameworks governing workplace conflicts requires a keen understanding to ensure that actions taken are both compliant and ethical.

Employment law forms the backbone of fair workplace practices, setting clear boundaries for acceptable behavior. Title VII of the Civil Rights Act of 1964 stands as a cornerstone, prohibiting discrimination based on sex, race, color, national origin, and religion. It mandates that employers cannot discriminate in terms of work conditions, privileges, or compensation. This law ensures that all employees have the right to a workplace free from discrimination and harassment. Similarly, the Occupational Safety and Health (OSHA) Act of 1970 demands that employers provide a safe working environment, addressing issues like proper sanitary conditions and protection from workplace hazards. These laws collectively create a framework that protects employees' rights and safety, guiding managers in conflict resolution processes.

Staying within these legal boundaries is not just a matter of compliance but a safeguard against potential repercussions. Noncompliance can lead to severe legal consequences, including lawsuits, fines, and damage to an organization's reputation. Discriminatory practices, whether intentional or not, can result in significant liabilities. For example, a female crane operator faced discrimination due to inadequate sanitary facilities, violating OSHA regulations. These situations highlight the need for managers to be vigilant in upholding legal standards, ensuring that workplace policies do not inadvertently harm employees or expose the organization to legal risks.

Recognizing when legal considerations must be addressed is a critical skill for managers. Certain red flags indicate potential legal violations, such as complaints of harassment, discrimination, or unsafe working conditions. Managers should be equipped to identify these signs and take appropriate action. In cases where a harassment complaint arises, legal intervention may be necessary to protect the rights of all parties involved. Understanding the nuances of these situations allows managers to respond effectively, ensuring that conflicts are resolved in a manner that upholds both the law and the organization's values.

Consider a scenario where an employee files a complaint about a hostile work environment. The manager must navigate the situation with care, balancing the need to address the complaint while ensuring compliance with legal requirements. This involves conducting a thorough investigation, gathering evidence, and consulting with legal or HR professionals to determine the appropriate course of action. By approaching the situation with a clear understanding of the legal framework, managers can resolve conflicts in a way that protects the organization and its employees.

7.2 Ethical Decision-Making in Conflict Scenarios

Imagine a fast-paced office where decisions must be made quickly, yet fairly. As a manager, the ethical landscape is one you navigate daily, especially when resolving conflicts. Ethics in conflict resolution is not merely a guideline, but a vital component of ensuring fairness and justice. It involves balancing organizational goals with individual rights, a task that often requires walking a fine line.

To tackle ethical dilemmas effectively, a structured approach is invaluable. The PLUS Ethical Decision-Making Model offers a reliable framework. This model helps in identifying stakeholders, evaluating options, and weighing consequences, ensuring decisions align with organizational values and legal standards. By integrating ethical guidelines and codes of conduct, managers can navigate complex situations with greater clarity. These tools serve as a compass, guiding managers through the murky waters of ethical conflicts. They help in maintaining a focus on integrity and fairness, even when the path isn't clear. By adopting such a structured approach, you can ensure that your decisions reflect the core values of your organization and respect the rights of all parties involved.

Conflicts of interest can arise, particularly when decision-makers have personal stakes in the outcomes. These situations demand transparency and honesty, ensuring that personal biases do not compromise fairness. Balancing transparency with confidentiality is another common dilemma. While openness is crucial for trust and accountability, it's equally important to protect sensitive information. This balance requires discretion and judgment, ensuring that confidentiality is maintained without sacrificing the transparency necessary for collective trust. Addressing these challenges involves a commitment to ethical principles, ensuring that decisions are made with due regard for all parties involved.

Consider a situation where a manager must handle a whistleblower complaint. The ethical implications are significant, as the complaint could involve issues of fraud or misconduct. In this case, it's essential to ensure fair treatment of the whistleblower while protecting the organization's interests. This requires a careful evaluation of the complaint, maintaining confidentiality, and ensuring that the investigation is thorough and unbiased. By upholding ethical standards, the manager can navigate the complexities of the situation, ensuring that justice is served and the organization's integrity is maintained. This example underscores the importance of ethical decision-making in conflict resolution, highlighting how it leads to fair and just outcomes.

Reflection Section: Ethical Decision-Making in Practice

Reflect on a recent decision you made that involved ethical considerations. Did you use a structured model to guide your decision? How did you balance organizational goals with individual rights? Consider how you might apply the PLUS Ethical Decision-Making Model to future conflicts. Reflecting on these questions can deepen your understanding of ethical decision-making and enhance your ability to navigate complex situations.

Ethical decision-making is not just an abstract concept; it's a practical tool that guides managers in resolving conflicts with integrity. By incorporating ethical frameworks and tools into your decision-making process, you can ensure that your actions align with organizational values and uphold the principles of fairness and justice. This approach strengthens your leadership and fosters a culture of trust and accountability within your team. As you continue to engage with these ethical considerations, you contribute to a workplace environment where fairness and integrity are the cornerstones of decision-making.

7.3 Ensuring Compliance with Organizational Policies

In the realm of conflict resolution, adherence to organizational policies is pivotal for maintaining consistency and fairness. Policies serve as the bedrock upon which conflict resolution procedures are built, providing a structured approach to managing disputes. They outline the standards and expectations for behavior, ensuring that all employees are aware of their rights and responsibilities. By following these guidelines, managers can navigate conflicts with clarity, ensuring that resolutions are not only fair, but also aligned with the organization's values and objectives. This consistency fosters a sense of trust and reliability, as employees know that conflicts will be handled in a manner that is both predictable and just. When policies are adhered to, they create an environment where conflicts are less likely to escalate, as employees understand the framework within which disputes will be resolved. This understanding reduces anxiety and confusion, paving the way for more efficient and effective conflict management.

To ensure policy compliance, managers must adopt proactive strategies that integrate policy adherence into everyday conflict resolution practices. Regular policy training sessions for managers are an essential tool. These sessions provide managers with the knowledge and skills needed to apply policies consistently and effectively. They also offer an opportunity to discuss real-world scenarios, exploring how policies can be applied in various contexts. By engaging in these training sessions, managers can enhance their understanding of the policies and procedures, ensuring they are well-equipped to handle conflicts in accordance with organizational standards. Additionally, implementing checklists for policy alignment during conflict resolution can serve as a valuable resource. These checklists guide managers through the resolution process, ensuring that all aspects of the policy are considered and adhered to. By using these tools, managers can maintain a high level of compliance, ensuring that conflicts are resolved in a manner that is fair and consistent with organizational expectations.

Despite the benefits of policy compliance, challenges can arise that hinder its effectiveness. One significant obstacle is the presence of outdated policies that no longer align with the current organizational culture or industry standards. These outdated policies can create confusion and inconsistency, as managers struggle to apply guidelines that are no longer relevant or effective. To address this issue, organizations must regularly review and update their policies, ensuring they remain aligned with the evolving needs and values of the organization. Another challenge is the lack of awareness among employees and managers regarding the policies and procedures. This lack of awareness can lead to unintentional noncompliance, as individuals are unaware of the guidelines that govern conflict resolution. To combat this, organizations must prioritize communication and education, ensuring that all employees are familiar with the policies and understand their importance. By fostering a culture of awareness and understanding, organizations can enhance policy compliance, reducing the likelihood of conflicts and ensuring that disputes are resolved in accordance with organizational standards.

Consider this case study, where a conflict arises due to the misuse of email within the organization. In this case, adherence to IT policies plays a crucial role in resolving the dispute. By following the established guidelines for email usage, the manager can address the issue effectively, ensuring that the resolution is fair and consistent with organizational expectations. The policies provide a clear framework for addressing the misuse, outlining the steps that must be taken to investigate and resolve the conflict. By adhering to these guidelines, the manager can ensure that the resolution is not only compliant with organizational standards, but also fair and just for all parties involved. This adherence to policy resolves the conflict and reinforces the importance of policy compliance within the organization, signaling to employees that violations will be addressed promptly and fairly. This consistency builds trust and confidence, as employees know that conflicts will be managed in a manner that is both predictable and equitable, fostering a work environment where fairness and accountability are paramount.

7.4 Protecting Confidentiality in Disputes

Within the intricate landscape of conflict management, maintaining confidentiality is pivotal, serving as the foundation upon which trust and integrity are built. When conflicts arise, employees must feel that their concerns will be handled with discretion and respect. This assurance encourages openness, making individuals more likely to bring issues forward without fear of backlash or exposure. A workplace where confidentiality is prioritized fosters a culture of trust, allowing team members to speak candidly about problems. Without this trust, potential issues may remain hidden, festering into larger disputes that could have been resolved earlier. The act of safeguarding sensitive information is not merely about maintaining privacy; it is about creating a safe space where employees feel valued and respected.

To ensure confidentiality, specific strategies must be implemented with diligence. One effective approach is the use of confidentiality agreements. These agreements serve as formal commitments to keep all discussions and information related to the conflict private. By having parties involved sign these agreements, managers can reinforce the importance of discretion and set clear expectations. Another critical strategy is the secure handling of sensitive documents. This involves storing physical documents in locked cabinets and using password-protected files for digital information. It's essential to limit access to these documents only to individuals who are directly involved in the resolution process. By controlling who can view this sensitive information, the risk of unauthorized disclosure is significantly reduced. These measures collectively create an environment where confidentiality is not just a policy, but a practice ingrained in the organization's culture.

One of the most common issues is the accidental disclosure of information during open discussions. In meetings where multiple parties are involved, it's easy for sensitive details to be inadvertently shared. To prevent this, managers must establish clear guidelines about what can and cannot be discussed in open forums. Another challenge is the temptation to share information with colleagues out of a desire to seek advice or validation. Managers must resist this temptation and instead rely on formal channels, such as HR or legal advisors, for guidance. By doing so, they can ensure that confidentiality is upheld and trust is maintained. Managers must remain vigilant, consistently reinforcing the importance of confidentiality to prevent breaches that could compromise the integrity of the resolution process.

7.5 Documenting Conflict Resolution Efforts

A manager's day is often filled with meetings, tasks, and inevitably, conflicts. Amidst this whirlwind, the importance of documentation in conflict resolution sometimes fades into the background. Yet, thorough documentation serves as a critical pillar in managing disputes effectively, providing a clear record that supports accountability and transparency. When conflicts arise, having a documented history allows managers to trace the progression of events, understand the context, and make informed decisions. This record is indispensable, especially when legal or organizational scrutiny comes into play. Documentation protects the organization by demonstrating due diligence and serves as a historical reference, offering insights into recurring issues and patterns that can inform future strategies. By maintaining comprehensive records, managers can ensure that all parties are held accountable, reducing the likelihood of disputes reoccurring and fostering a culture of responsibility and transparency.

Creating accurate and comprehensive documentation requires a strategic approach, emphasizing consistency and attention to detail. One effective method is using standardized forms and templates. These tools provide a structured format for capturing essential information, ensuring that all relevant details are recorded consistently. By standardizing the documentation process, managers can avoid the pitfalls of incomplete or inconsistent records, which can lead to misunderstandings or misrepresentations. Key details such as dates, involved parties, and outcomes must be meticulously recorded. This practice ensures that all pertinent information is captured and also facilitates easy retrieval and analysis when needed. By maintaining detailed records, managers can quickly access the information required to address conflicts, make decisions, and implement effective resolutions. This meticulous approach to documentation enhances the overall efficiency and effectiveness of conflict resolution efforts.

Despite the clear benefits, documenting conflicts presents challenges that managers must navigate carefully. One potential issue is the risk of incomplete records. In the fast-paced environment of modern workplaces, it's easy for details to be overlooked or omitted. To combat this, managers must prioritize thoroughness, ensuring that every aspect of the conflict is documented with precision. Another challenge is the potential for biased reporting. Personal biases can inadvertently influence how conflicts are recorded, leading to skewed or inaccurate accounts. To ensure objectivity and neutrality, managers must adopt an impartial approach, focusing on factual details and avoiding subjective interpretations. By maintaining a neutral stance, managers can create documentation that accurately reflects the situation, providing a reliable foundation for resolution efforts. This commitment to objectivity strengthens the integrity of the documentation and enhances the credibility and trustworthiness of the conflict resolution process.

Consider an instance where a performance issue arises within a team. A manager records detailed observations of incidents, noting specific behaviors, dates, and interactions. This comprehensive documentation provides a clear picture of the situation, allowing the manager to address the issue effectively. By presenting an objective account of events, the manager can engage the employee in a constructive conversation, focusing on finding solutions rather than assigning blame. This approach resolves the performance issue and reinforces the importance of documentation in supporting fair and effective conflict resolution. Through detailed documentation, managers can create an environment where conflicts are managed proactively, reducing the likelihood of escalation and fostering a culture of accountability and transparency.

EIGHT

Managing Remote and Hybrid Team Conflicts

Imagine an energetic virtual meeting with team members scattered across the globe. The meeting begins smoothly, but soon the screen freezes, voices overlap, and the once clear agenda becomes muddled. This scenario is all too familiar in the realm of remote work, where the absence of physical presence can lead to misunderstandings and communication challenges. As managers, you're tasked with overcoming these unique barriers to maintain effective team dynamics. In this chapter, we explore practical strategies to navigate the complexities of virtual communication, ensuring your team remains cohesive and productive despite the distance.

8.1 Effective Communication in Virtual Environments

Virtual communication presents distinct challenges. In the absence of physical cues, messages can easily be misinterpreted. A seemingly benign email might be perceived as curt or dismissive due to its tone. Without the nuance of facial expressions or body language, intentions can be misconstrued. Video call quality further complicates matters. Poor connectivity can distort voices or freeze frames, leaving participants unsure of each other's reactions or sentiments. The result is a communication landscape fraught with potential pitfalls, where even the most straightforward message can lead to confusion.

To enhance virtual communication, structured meeting agendas are essential. Clear agendas provide focus and predictability, guiding discussions and ensuring no time is wasted on tangents. Before organizing a virtual meeting, ensure there is a clear purpose and communicate it to participants. When possible, use video during calls to add non-verbal context. Seeing a colleague's smile or nod can provide reassurance and clarity, fostering a sense of connection that audio alone cannot achieve. Additionally, limit meeting invites to essential participants to maintain efficiency, aiming for no more than ten attendees. These strategies help create an environment where team members feel engaged and understood, despite the physical distance.

Clarity and brevity are paramount in virtual settings. Messages should be concise and direct, avoiding jargon or complex language that might lead to misunderstandings. When composing emails, consider the reader's perspective. Use bullet points to highlight key messages, making it easier for recipients to grasp the main points at a glance. This format enhances comprehension and respects the reader's time, allowing them to quickly absorb and respond to essential information. By prioritizing clear communication, you can mitigate the risk of misinterpretation and keep your team aligned.

Consider an example of a virtual project update meeting where visual aids played a crucial role. During the meeting, presenters used slides with a maximum of five bullet points and five words per bullet to convey complex information succinctly. This approach maintained the audience's attention and ensured that key messages were understood. By breaking down complex messages into digestible parts, presenters kept the discussion focused and productive. The meeting's success lay in its structure, demonstrating how thoughtful planning and execution can overcome the challenges of virtual communication.

Interactive Exercise: Enhancing Virtual Communication

Consider conducting a virtual communication workshop with your team. Encourage participants to practice writing clear and concise emails using bullet points, and role-play virtual meetings with structured agendas. Provide feedback on their communication style, emphasizing areas for improvement. This exercise fosters awareness and skill development, equipping your team to navigate the complexities of virtual communication with confidence.

As we delve into the nuances of managing remote and hybrid teams, remember that the key lies in adapting and evolving your communication strategies. By embracing these tools and techniques, you can foster a virtual environment where collaboration thrives and conflicts are minimized.

8.2 Addressing Miscommunications in Remote Teams

In the complex world of remote work, miscommunication stands as a formidable challenge for managers. Picture a scenario where a team member in New York schedules a meeting at 9 a.m., unaware that their colleague in Sydney will be joining at midnight. Time zone differences like these often lead to missed meetings and frustration. Without careful coordination, these variations can wreak havoc on team schedules and productivity. It's crucial to be aware of these differences and plan accordingly. Use tools like world clocks and calendar apps that automatically adjust for time zones, ensuring everyone has a clear understanding of meeting times. Clearly communicating and confirming these details beforehand can prevent unnecessary confusion and stress.

Cultural nuances in communication styles further complicate interactions. Directness in one culture might be perceived as rudeness in another, while indirect communication may seem evasive or unclear. These subtle differences can lead to misinterpretations and conflicts if not managed thoughtfully. Managers should foster an environment where team members feel comfortable expressing their communication preferences and concerns. Encourage openness about cultural norms and styles, allowing for adjustments that accommodate everyone's needs. This understanding and respect for diversity can bridge gaps and enhance communication across your team.

To address these challenges, establishing standard communication protocols is vital. These protocols serve as a foundation for clear and consistent interactions, reducing the likelihood of misunderstandings. For instance, agreeing on preferred communication channels for different types of messages—such as using emails for formal updates and instant messaging for quick questions—can streamline communication and prevent important information from getting lost. Implementing feedback loops is another effective strategy. Encourage team members to ask for clarification or provide feedback when they are unsure about a message's intent. This practice clarifies communication and empowers team members to take an active role in preventing miscommunication.

Regular check-ins play a pivotal role in maintaining alignment and reducing miscommunications. Weekly team check-ins offer a platform for discussing ongoing projects, aligning on priorities, and addressing any concerns that may arise. These touchpoints provide an opportunity to clarify goals and ensure everyone is on the same page. During these meetings, encourage open dialogue and invite team members to share updates or potential issues. This proactive approach fosters a culture of transparency and collaboration, minimizing the risk of miscommunication and promoting a cohesive team environment.

Reflection Section: Evaluating Communication Practices

Take a moment to reflect on your team's current communication practices. Are there areas where miscommunications frequently occur? Consider how time zones and cultural differences might be impacting interactions. Evaluate whether your team has established clear communication protocols and if regular check-ins are part of your routine. Use this reflection to identify potential improvements and implement strategies that enhance clarity and understanding within your team. By embracing these strategies, you can create a remote work environment where communication flows effortlessly.

8.3 Building Trust and Rapport Online

In the digital age, building trust in virtual teams is more crucial than ever. Trust is the glue that holds a team together, significantly impacting both cohesion and performance. When trust is present, team members collaborate more effectively, share ideas openly, and work towards common goals with enthusiasm. Studies consistently show that teams with high levels of trust achieve higher productivity and innovation. In a virtual setting, where physical cues are absent, this trust must be nurtured deliberately. It requires an intentional effort to create a sense of closeness and camaraderie, even when screens and miles separate team members.

To foster trust remotely, consider incorporating virtual team-building exercises into your routine. These activities, though executed online, can effectively break the ice and encourage team members to connect on a personal level. Simple exercises like "Four Facts and a Fib" or virtual escape rooms can bring team members together, highlighting shared interests and experiences. Another powerful tool is the use of informal communication channels, such as chat groups or virtual lounges. These spaces allow team members to engage in casual conversations, share jokes, and discuss non-work-related topics, much like they would in an office break room. These interactions build rapport, humanize team members, and create an environment where employees feel comfortable and valued.

Regular one-on-one meetings are another strategy to build trust and understanding. These sessions provide an opportunity to address individual concerns, offer personalized feedback, and discuss career development. By taking the time to understand each team member's unique challenges and aspirations, you demonstrate genuine care and investment in their success. These meetings are a chance to listen, to offer support, and to build a deeper connection that transcends the virtual divide. They also allow you to gain insights into team dynamics and identify potential issues before they escalate into conflicts.

Initial skepticism is common, especially among new team members who have not yet had the chance to build personal connections. Overcoming this skepticism requires consistency and transparency. Be open about your intentions and encourage team members to do the same. Share your own experiences and encourage others to share theirs. This openness can create a foundation of trust that grows stronger over time. It's important to be patient and persistent, as building trust is a gradual process that requires continuous effort and reinforcement.

Consider the example of a distributed team that organized virtual coffee breaks to enhance camaraderie. These informal gatherings provided a space for team members to chat about their weekends, discuss hobbies, or simply enjoy a cup of coffee together. Over time, these moments of connection fostered a sense of belonging and trust, transforming the team dynamics. Team members felt more comfortable reaching out for help, collaborating on projects, and sharing their ideas. The virtual coffee breaks, though simple, laid the groundwork for a cohesive and supportive team environment. This initiative illustrates how creativity and intentionality in building rapport can lead to meaningful connections, even in a virtual world.

8.4 Strategies for Remote Conflict Mediation

Mediating conflicts in a remote setting presents unique challenges and opportunities for managers. Without the benefit of face-to-face interaction, traditional mediation skills require adaptation to a virtual environment. However, the core principles of mediation remain unchanged: facilitating communication, fostering understanding, and guiding conflicting parties towards a mutually agreeable solution. In a virtual setting, the role of a neutral facilitator becomes even more critical. The facilitator acts as an impartial guide who ensures that both parties have the opportunity to express their perspectives. This neutrality helps maintain balance, encourages open dialogue, and fosters trust between all participants. By embracing technology, managers can create a structured and effective mediation environment that mirrors the success of in-person interactions.

A step-by-step guide for conducting remote mediation begins with thorough preparation. Prior to the mediation session, gather information through pre-meeting surveys. These surveys allow each party to express their concerns, identify key issues, and set expectations for the mediation process. This preparation helps the facilitator understand the conflict's dynamics and anticipate potential areas of agreement or contention. Next, establish clear ground rules for the virtual mediation session. Ensure that all participants understand and agree to these rules, which may include guidelines for respectful communication, equal speaking time, and confidentiality. By setting the stage for a respectful and focused discussion, these rules create a safe and productive environment for conflict resolution.

Technology plays a vital role in remote mediation by providing tools that enhance communication and maintain accountability. Breakout rooms, a feature available on many video conferencing platforms, allow for private discussions between the mediator and individual parties. These sessions provide a space for participants to speak candidly and explore sensitive topics without the pressure of a group setting. Additionally, recording the mediation session can serve as a valuable tool for accountability and review. It allows parties to revisit the discussions and agreements, ensuring that all commitments are clear and understood. However, it is essential to obtain consent from all participants before recording, as this practice must align with privacy considerations and legal requirements.

Successful remote mediation can be illustrated through the example of a customer service team resolving a dispute over resource allocation. The conflict arose when different departments competed for limited resources, leading to frustration and tension. The manager initiated a virtual mediation session, beginning with pre-meeting surveys to gather each department's perspectives and concerns. During the mediation, the manager facilitated a structured discussion, allowing each party to articulate their needs and proposed solutions. Breakout rooms provided a space for private conversations, where individuals could express sensitive issues without fear of judgment. Through open communication and mutual understanding, the parties reached a consensus on resource allocation that satisfied all involved. The mediation resolved the immediate conflict and strengthened interdepartmental relationships, fostering collaboration for future projects.

In conducting remote mediation, managers must remain adaptable, responsive, and committed to creating a fair and open dialogue. By leveraging technology and adhering to structured processes, you can guide your team through conflicts with confidence, transforming challenges into opportunities for growth and understanding.

8.5 Technology Tools for Conflict Management

Digital tools facilitate communication and help with conflict resolution, offering a structured approach to track and manage disagreements. Software that welcomes collaboration stands out as a game-changer, particularly for conflict tracking. These platforms allow managers to record and monitor the progress of conflict resolution efforts, ensuring that nothing slips through the cracks. With features that enable document sharing, task assignment, and real-time updates, collaboration tools provide a transparent space where team members can see the status of ongoing conflicts. This transparency is crucial for maintaining accountability and ensuring that everyone is on the same page, reducing the chances of misunderstandings or unresolved issues festering over time. Furthermore, by centralizing communication and documentation, these tools streamline the conflict resolution process, allowing managers to focus on finding solutions rather than getting bogged down in administrative details.

A variety of technology tools are available to aid in conflict management, each designed to address specific needs within a team. Platforms like Slack and Microsoft Teams facilitate real-time communication, offering channels where team members can discuss issues as they arise. These tools provide a space for quick exchanges and immediate feedback, helping to resolve minor conflicts before they escalate. For task tracking, project management tools such as Trello or Asana are invaluable. They allow managers to assign tasks related to conflict resolution, set deadlines, and monitor progress. This organized approach ensures that all parties involved understand their responsibilities and can work towards resolution efficiently. The visual nature of these platforms, with boards and cards representing different tasks, makes it easy for everyone to see the big picture and their role within it. By integrating these tools into daily operations, managers can create a more structured and proactive approach to conflict management.

Choosing the right tools for your team is a critical step in leveraging technology effectively. It's essential to select tools that align with your team's size, needs, and the complexity of tasks you undertake. For smaller teams, a simple communication app might suffice, while larger teams with more intricate needs might benefit from a robust project management system. Evaluate each tool based on its features, ease of use, and integration capabilities with other software your team already uses. Consider conducting a needs assessment to determine which tools will best support your team's conflict management efforts. This assessment should involve input from team members to ensure that the chosen tools meet their needs and preferences. By carefully selecting tools that fit your team's dynamics, you can enhance communication, streamline workflows, and ultimately improve your team's ability to manage conflicts effectively.

Consider a scenario where a marketing team utilized a shared document platform to collaborate on campaign strategies. The team, spread across different locations, faced challenges in coordinating their efforts and sharing ideas. By using a centralized platform, they could upload documents, provide feedback, and make real-time edits, all within a single interface. This open access to information allowed team members to stay informed about each other's contributions, minimizing misunderstandings and fostering a sense of unity. The platform also included a comment feature, enabling team members to discuss potential conflicts directly on the document, ensuring that issues were addressed promptly. As a result, the team successfully launched a cohesive campaign that reflected diverse perspectives and expertise. This example highlights the transformative power of technology in managing remote conflicts, showcasing how the right tools can bridge gaps and facilitate effective collaboration.

A Chance to Pay It Forward

As you turn the last pages of this book, please take a moment to hold the door open for someone else – for another manager that may be experiencing conflicts with their team.

Simply by sharing one or two sentences about your own experiences with conflict resolution, you'll show new readers where they can find the tools they need to build stronger, more cohesive teams.

Please scan the QR code to leave a review.

Thank you for your support. We're all on our own leadership journey, but every bit of insight we share can make a significant impact on shaping healthier, more collaborative workplaces.

Conclusion

As we reach the end of this book, I hope that the journey we've embarked on together has been insightful and empowering. The primary goal of this book was to equip you, as a manager, with practical skills to prevent, manage, and resolve conflicts in the workplace. Conflict is an inevitable part of any professional environment, but with the right tools and mindset, it can be transformed into an opportunity for growth, collaboration, and innovation.

Throughout the chapters, we've delved into different aspects of conflict management. We began with the foundation of effective communication, emphasizing the power of active listening, empathy, and assertive communication. These skills are crucial in understanding and addressing the needs of your team, ensuring that everyone feels heard and respected.

We then explored the realm of emotional intelligence, a vital component in recognizing and managing emotions during conflicts. By understanding emotional triggers and practicing self-regulation, you can maintain composure and guide your team through challenging situations with empathy and clarity.

Followed by structured conflict resolution frameworks, offering you a step-by-step approach to identifying root causes and implementing effective solutions. These frameworks are designed to provide clarity and consistency, ensuring that conflicts are addressed systematically and fairly.

Mediation and negotiation skills were also highlighted, showing how you can facilitate discussions and find win-win solutions. By maintaining neutrality and focusing on shared interests, you can foster a collaborative environment where conflicts become opportunities for creative problem-solving.

Building a conflict-positive culture was another key focus, encouraging open dialogue and constructive criticism. This culture enhances team dynamics and drives innovation by leveraging diverse perspectives.

When dealing with difficult personalities, we provided strategies to manage and resolve conflicts with tact and understanding. Recognizing different personality types and adapting your approach can transform potential adversities into productive relationships.

Finally, we addressed legal and ethical considerations, ensuring that your conflict management practices align with organizational policies and legal standards. This ensures compliance and fosters a workplace that upholds fairness and integrity.

The key takeaway for you as a manager is that conflict management is a multifaceted skill set. It's not just about resolving disputes—it's about leading with empathy, fostering a positive culture, and turning challenges into opportunities for growth. By applying the skills and strategies discussed, you can enhance your leadership capabilities, improve team cohesion, and drive profes-sional development in your organization.

I encourage you to take action. Reflect on what you've learned and implement these strategies in your daily interactions. Practice active listening, embrace diversity, and lead with empathy. Your role as a manager is pivotal in creating a harmonious and produc-tive work environment. I hope that the insights shared here will have a lasting impact on you and your team.

Remember, conflict management is an ongoing journey. I urge you to continue learning and seeking out resources that enhance your skills. Attend workshops, read widely, and engage in reflective practices. By committing to continuous improvement, you can ensure that your conflict management abilities remain sharp and relevant.

Thank you for taking this journey with me. I am confident that, with dedication and practice, you will transform your workplace into a thriving environment where every voice is heard, and every conflict is an opportunity for growth.

Amber Preston

References

Acrolinx. (2024, August 30). *Empathetic communication: Why is it important at work?* Retrieved from https://www.acrolinx.com/blog/empathetic-communication-why-is-it-important-at-work/

Aurora Training Advantage. (n.d.). *Conflict resolution: A quality found in effective leaders.* Retrieved from https://auroratrainingadvantage.com/leadership/conflict-resolution-leadership-quality/

CA Consumer Law APC. (2023, September 26). *Why neutrality is crucial in mediation.* Retrieved from https://caconsumerlaw.com/blog/why-neutrality-is-crucial-in-mediation/

Coursera. (2024, October 25). *Assertive communication: Definition, examples, and tips.* Retrieved from https://www.coursera.org/articles/assertive-communication

CTR Institute. (n.d.). *10 strategies for dealing with passive-aggressive people.* Retrieved from https://ctrinstitute.com/blog/10-strategies-for-dealing-with-passive-aggressive-people/

Ethics.org. (n.d.). *The PLUS ethical decision making model.* Retrieved from https://www.ethics.org/resources/free-toolkit/decision-making-model/

Euronext. (2025, January 9). *8 steps to develop a strong compliance strategy.* Retrieved from https://www.corporateservices.euronext.com/blog/compliance/strategy

Exude Inc. (2020, July 23). *Positive conflict resolution in remote work environments.* Retrieved from https://www.exudeinc.com/blog/positive-conflict-resolution-in-remote-work-environments/

Forbes Human Resources Council. (2019, November 5). *12 dispute mediation techniques for managers.* Retrieved from https://www.forbes.com/councils/forbeshumanresourcescouncil/2019/11/05/12-dispute-mediation-techniques-for-managers/

Harvard Business Review. (2023, October). *What we get wrong about empathic leadership.* Retrieved from https://hbr.org/2023/10/what-we-get-wrong-about-empathic-leadership

Huthwaite International. (n.d.). *How to master virtual communications: 10 expert tips.* Retrieved from https://www.huthwaiteinternational.com/blog/effective-virtual-communication

Indeed. (2024, November 4). *Active listening in the workplace: How it makes you a better manager.* Retrieved from https://www.indeed.com/hire/c/info/active-listening-in-the-workplace-for-managers

JAMS Pathways. (2024, September 6). *Addressing conflict in a remote setting: Strategies for success.* Retrieved from https://www.jamspathways.com/news-insights/addressing-conflict-in-a-remote-setting-strategies-for-success

JAMS Pathways. (n.d.). *Workplace conflict resolution success stories & case studies.* Retrieved from https://www.jamspathways.com/successstories

Kurter, H. L. (2022, January 27). *3 ways to best handle aggressive people in the workplace.* Retrieved from https://www.forbes.com/sites/heidilynnekurter/2022/01/27/3-ways-to-best-handle-aggressive-people-in-the-workplace/

Law Birdie. (2023, July 30). *Workplace conflict and employment laws.* Retrieved from https://lawbirdie.com/workplace-conflict-and-employment-laws/

LeaderFactor. (2024, October 16). *Psychological safe space.* Retrieved from https://www.leaderfactor.com/learn/psychological-safe-space

Life Coach Training. (n.d.). *The importance of emotional intelligence in conflict resolution.* Retrieved from https://lifecoachtraining.co/the-importance-of-emotional-intelligence-in-conflict-resolution/

Mayo Clinic. (2023, December 23). *Resilience: Build skills to endure hardship.* Retrieved from https://www.mayoclinic.org/tests-procedures/resilience-training/in-depth/resilience/art-20046311

Mediation Training Institute. (n.d.). *Conflict competence.* Retrieved from https://www.mediationworks.com/conflict-competence/

Mind Tools. (n.d.). *8 ways to improve self-regulation - "Feed your good wolf".* Retrieved from https://www.mindtools.com/aunxs99/8-ways-to-improve-self-regulation

Mind Tools. (n.d.). *Virtual team-building exercises.* Retrieved from https://www.mindtools.com/a3pfy3c/virtual-team-building-exercises

Psychology Today. (2024, March 5). *9 steps for successfully managing conflict with a narcissist.* Retrieved from https://www.psychologytoday.com/us/blog/childhood-narcissism/202403/9-steps-for-successfully-managing-conflict-with-a-narcissist

SHRM. (2024, September 19). *Why HR confidentiality is essential for protecting employees.* Retrieved from https://www.shrm.org/topics-tools/tools/hr-answers/confidentiality-critical-to-human-resources

Siragusa, T. (2023, October 16). *Redefining conflict resolution: The design thinking way.* Retrieved from https://tulliosiragusa.com/resolving-conflict/

Speakeasy. (2024, May 14). *The importance of non-verbal communication skills in conflict resolution.* Retrieved from https://www.speakeasyinc.com/the-importance-of-non-verbal-communication-skills-in-conflict-resolution/

The Collective. (2023, February 20). *Innovate through conflict: A tech leadership guide.* Retrieved from https://www.jointhecollective.com/article/conflict-resolution-and-innovation--turning-disagreements-into-opportunities/

The Maker Group. (n.d.). *Benefits and strategies for a successful win-win negotiation.* Retrieved from https://themakergroup.com/win-win-negotiation/

The Myers-Briggs Company. (2020, March 13). *Myers-Briggs Type Indicator® conflict style report.* Retrieved from https://www.themyersbriggs.com/en-US/Products-and-Services/-/media/myers-briggs/files/sample-reports/smp261161.pdf

Versed. (n.d.). *Uncover conflict roots with five whys.* Retrieved from https://www.versed.uk/blog/uncover-conflict-roots-with-five-whys

Vistage. (2023, May 12). *What are the best negotiation strategies?* Retrieved from https://www.vistage.com/research-center/business-growth-strategy/six-successful-strategies-for-negotiation/

Voltage Control. (2024, February 13). *Navigating conflict and fostering open communication.* Retrieved from https://voltagecontrol.com/articles/navigating-conflict-and-fostering-open-communication-a-collaborative-leadership-approach/